ON ARISTOTLE

ALSO BY ALAN RYAN

ON ARISTOTLE

Saving Politics from Philosophy

ALAN RYAN

LIVERIGHT PUBLISHING CORPORATION

A Division of W. W. Norton & Company
New York / London

For information about permission to
reproduce selections from this book,
write to Permissions, Liveright Publishing Corporation,
a division of W. W. Norton & Company, Inc.,
500 Fifth Avenue, New York, NY 10110

For information about special discounts for bulk
purchases, please contact W. W. Norton Special Sales at
specialsales@wwnorton.com or 800-233-4830

Manufacturing by Courier Westford
Book design by Ellen Cipriano
Production manager: Anna Oler

ISBN 978-0-87140-706-1

Liveright Publishing Corporation
500 Fifth Avenue, New York, N.Y. 10110
www.wwnorton.com

W. W. Norton & Company Ltd.
Castle House, 75/76 Wells Street, London W1T 3QT

1 2 3 4 5 6 7 8 9 0

CONTENTS

PREFACE

❦

IN THE INTRODUCTION TO *On Politics*, I suggested that one measure of the book's success would be the readers who went and read the works of the authors I discussed. Some readers suggested that I might encourage them to do so by taking chapters of *On Politics* and adding to them substantial extracts from the works I hoped they would read. What follows is exactly that, with a short introduction to provide some of the context that the chapter's original placement in *On Politics* would have provided. As before, I am grateful to Bob Weil and William Menaker at Liveright, as well as to the Norton production team, for their help in making an author's life as easy as it can plausibly be made.

CHRONOLOGY

of Epaminondas disables Theban attempts at hegemony

360   *Republic* written by Plato

359   Philip II becomes king of Macedon

356   Birth of Alexander the Great

347   *Laws* written shortly before the death of Plato; Aristotle leaves Athens

343   Aristotle becomes tutor to Alexander

338   Philip II defeats Greek alliance at Chaeronea, becomes hegemon over Greece

336   Philip of Macedon murdered; Alexander prepares invasion of Persia

335   Aristotle returns to Athens and founds the Lyceum

323   Alexander dies at Babylon

322   Aristotle dies on island of Euboea; Athenian fleet defeated at Battle of Amorgos; Demosthenes commits suicide

INTRODUCTION

❧

ARISTOTLE WROTE HIS TREATISE on political systems during the last years of Athenian democracy, or more exactly, during the last years in which Athens existed as a fully independent sovereign state. Like many other Greek cities, Athens preserved democratic arrangements for managing its local affairs long after it had fallen under the control of the kingdom of Macedon and then of the successors of Alexander the Great. Indeed, the Athenians periodically attempted to recover their autonomy even after the Greek-speaking Mediterranean had been conquered by the Romans in the second century BCE; the last of these revolts ended with the city's being sacked by the forces of the Roman dictator Sulla in 86 BCE. During the fourth century BCE the rising power in the Greek world was the kingdom of Macedon. After the Battle of Chaeronea, in 338, when a Macedonian army led by Alexander the Great's father,

Philip II, defeated the combined forces of Athens and Thebes, Athens was forced to accept the authority of a Macedonian regent. The great orator Demosthenes made his name and imperiled his life by urging the Athenians to revolt against their subordination; the label "Philippic" has stuck to such speeches ever since. An opportunity arose when Alexander died in Babylon in 323, but when the Athenian navy encountered the Macedonian fleet at Amorgos in 322, it turned tail and fled to Athens; the rule of Alexander's regent, Antipater, was restored, Demosthenes committed suicide, and from then on Athens would be at the mercy of successive empires, first Hellenistic, then Roman, finally Ottoman. Nonetheless, Athens remained at the center of the philosophical world, and the teachers of Stoicism and Epicureanism never lacked for students; Platonism was taught in the Academy until 83 BCE, and the Academy was definitively suppressed only in 529 CE, by the emperor Justinian. For political purposes, however, Athens was a provincial city in empires whose fate was determined elsewhere. Not until the war of independence that began in 1821 was Greece liberated once more; the capital was initially established at Nauplia, and moved to Athens after 1834.

To place Aristotle in context, a brief sketch may be helpful of the rise and fall of the Athenian democracy, whose political "death" in 322 coincided all too neatly with Aristotle's own, and of the afterlife of Aristotle's broader philosophy and his *Politics* in particular. Athens was untypical of Greek city-states; it was much larger than others, with a population that is thought to have peaked before the Peloponnesian War at around 300,000, of whom some 100,000 were slaves and foreigners. Until the rise of Rome, the city itself with some 75,000 inhabitants was much larger than most other Mediterranean cities. As in all preindustrial societies, its inhabitants' energies were heavily devoted to physical survival; most free Athenians were farmers, either farming their own land with the assistance of a slave or two or farming the lands of richer Athenians who owned slaves and employed free laborers. But Athens was also a trading society; the soil of Attica did not produce enough corn to feed the entire population, and Athenian ships sailed to Egypt and to cities on the shores of the Black Sea for supplies; those with enough land for the purpose produced olive oil and wine for export. Later commentators, most famously Benjamin Constant, emphasized the importance of the fact that Athens was a "commercial" society, which they believed was a key influence in making Athens more hospitable to individual liberty in the modern sense than other ancient city-states. Pericles's famous funeral speech praises the Athenians for not looking askance at their neighbors merely because their tastes were different;

the contrast with Sparta is not spelled out, but is everywhere implied.

Like many ancient city-states, Athens was riven with social conflict. It was not simply a conflict of rich versus poor, even though there was much of that, and Aristotle treats the opposed interests of the "poor many" and the better-off as the fundamental division that a state must overcome by finding a just resolution of their competing demands on their society's resources and on access to political power. In Athens a three-way conflict was superimposed on the familiar division of better- and worse-off. Athenians who lived on the coast were often at odds with those who lived inland, and Athenians who lived in the city at odds with those who lived outside the city. The plays of Aristophanes are replete with depictions of simple countryfolk, some-times as objects of mockery, sometimes as the possess-ors of a common sense at odds with the follies of those who dwelt in the city. Finding a form of government that would keep the peace, secure everyone's property, and have enough fiscal capacity to find the resources to defend itself militarily, when necessary, was not easy; the attempt to establish a stable political and legal sys-tem broke down several times before the establishment of the democratic system in 508–506 that with inter-ruptions and modifications lasted until 322. It was only in the 1960s that the United States could claim to possess a longer-lasting democratic, or more strictly a "popular" republican, constitution. Like the United States, Athens established its constitution only in the aftermath of revolution; unlike the United States, Athens was a slave-owning society from start to finish.

The very early history of Athens is shrouded in mist and myth; the historian Herodotus complained that Athenian popular chronology was absurdly foreshortened, as if upper-class Athenians seriously believed that only a dozen generations separated them from heroes such as Hercules. In the absence of a uniform calendar, it is in fact very difficult to date events; records other than carved inscriptions were very vulnerable to destruction. Like most such states, Athens had been ruled by kings or small groups of the wellborn; the *archons*, either singly or later in a council of nine, reflected this history. The political history of Athens for our purposes may be said to begin with Solon's reforms of the very early sixth century. What the totality of Solon's reforms amounted to is not absolutely clear, but one aspect of his work is, and it casts light on some familiar tensions of the ancient, and not only the ancient, world. Solon was famous for abolishing debt slavery and for returning to Athens those who had been enslaved and sold abroad. He was the man who "overturned the markers." Small farmers were often obliged to take on debts to the well-off, and failure to repay whatever they had borrowed led to a form of slavery, running from something akin to serf-dom to chattel slavery. Stone markers indicated that the notional owner of the land in question was deeply indebted to someone else and held his land on a share-cropping tenure. He would be all but a serf and well on his way to debt slavery. Since the distinction between freedom and slavery was central to ancient politics, it is easy to imagine the hatred that poor farmers felt for such arrangements. Solon abolished sharecropping and canceled the debts that underlay it, and set limits to the amount of land that any one man could own.

He also appears to have seen the outlines of a per-manent political settlement, organizing the citizens in four classes according to their financial means and giv-ing some limited political rights to the lowest class, while confining eligibility for important public offices, both religious and judicial, to members of the better-off classes. This opened the highest offices to wealth, rather than birth alone, and guaranteed that the well-off would not be expropriated, while giving the poorer citi-zens a constitutional outlet for their grievances. Solon left Athens after his reforms and remained in self-imposed exile for a decade; his motives have variously been characterized as a fastidious desire not to turn himself into a tyrant by exercising power under rules that he had himself drawn up, a dislike of the idea of staying and watching his handiwork ruined by his bickering fellow citizens, and simple exhaustion in the face of incessant demands for favors from one person or group after another. His reforms satisfied nobody entirely, which was a sign of his evenhandedness; as so frequently since, hard-up farmers hoped for a wholesale land redistribution, and their creditors hoped to make fewer concessions to debtors than they were asked to do. The reforms did not survive. In 561 Athens fell under the rule of the tyrant Peisistratus. A "tyrant" in the eyes of the Greeks of that period was not someone who necessarily behaved badly; a tyrant was simply a sole ruler who had acquired power by other than constitutional means. Tyrants often took power when conflict was on the verge of turning into civil war; either the better-off or the worse-off might turn to a tyrant for protection. Peisistratus appears to have dealt equitably with his Athenian subjects and saved Athens from the horrors of protracted civil war; his rule was not unchallenged, but he was succeeded by his sons in 527, and the family governed Athens on and off until 510, when his surviving son was expelled by Athenian rebels assisted by a force from Sparta.

The Spartans had hoped to install an oligarchy friendly to themselves; instead, they helped to create their most formidable rival. Sparta was, and remained for another century, the strongest military force in Greece; its hoplite army, a highly trained, heavily armed infantry, which fought in the compact units known as phalanxes, was more than a match for that of other Greek states. Only in the fourth century did the Macedon phalanx prove to be its superior. However, Sparta was for the most part a stay-at-home state. Spartan men spent their time in military training; they lived austerely—Spartan food was notoriously bad—but the leisure required for their way of life meant that agricultural labor fell to the "helots," inhabitants of the surrounding countryisde who had been turned into serfs. Rebellion was rare, and the Spartans carried out periodic massacres of the helots to deter any thoughts of revolt. However, the knowledge that when they left Spartan territory, they were leaving behind a downtrodden and resentful peasantry was a deterrent to adventurousness.

The Athenian advantage lay in two things. The sea was Athens's natural element. For much of the fifth century, the Athenian navy was mistress of the Aegean, better trained and better commanded than any other. Athenian democracy and the Athenian navy reinforced each other. In all ancient city-states, citizen status was tied to a man's ability to serve in war; a periodic census would reveal the resources a man had to arm and support himself; status and political authority very closely followed wealth. However, navies needed rowers, and rowers did not need the heavy and expensive equipment of a hoplite soldier, so city-states that relied on their navies were more likely to be democratic, Athens above all. When Cleisthenes established a democratic constitution in 508–506, he enfranchised the lowest of the census classes, the *thetes*, who provided the rowers in the Athenian navy. His other great innovation was to resolve the conflicts between different parts of Athens by allocating every citizen to a deme, the name of which suggests a tribe, but which was essentially a grouping whose members were drawn from a diversity of geographical locations. The ten units were the basis for membership of the Assembly and public offices. The other great advantage was Athenian intelligence. This is not to suggest that Athenians were innately any more intelligent than other Greeks or anyone else; but the life of Athens was such as to put a premium on quick wits and imagination. Here, too, democracy reinforced one of its own supports. Commerce, of course, required intelligence and imagination; Athens invented many of the instruments of trade that were reinvented by the Italian city-states of medieval Europe, among them forms of insurance for cargoes and ships. The Athenians were also a very litigious people, and anyone with resources to protect needed to know how to make the best possible case in a court of law. This is not to say that the Athenian legal system would strike a modern observer favorably; there were no public prosecutors, and cases both civil and criminal had to be brought by individuals with an interest in the matter. Later, this requirement was confined to cases of homicide; someone who was neither a slave nor survived by living relatives would find his murder unprosecuted. The accuser stood to gain a proportion of any fine that was levied, so the incentives to malicious prosecution were many; the deterrent was the heavy penalty if a jury concluded that the prosecution was without merit or brought ultra vires.

The Athenian Assembly was a debating forum. The ability to sway the Assembly for good or ill was a highly prized asset. The Sophists, whom Plato rarely missed an opportunity to condemn as a social menace, taught the art of persuasive public speaking; Plato's dialogue *Gorgias* is perhaps the sharpest and most famous of his attacks on rhetoric, the victim in this case being the Sophist Gorgias, represented here as someone who would teach upper-class young men how to make the better case appear the worse and the worse case the better. Socrates demolishes Gorgias's claim to teach wisdom, and denounces rhetoric as a skill of the same kind as that of the purveyors of sweetmeats: it gives instant gratification but is ruinous to the health, in this case the moral health of the political community. It is the skill of the "pander" or pimp. Plato, of course, was one of history's sharpest critics of democracy. Nonetheless, it is well to remember that the Athenian democracy was far from liberal in many of its attitudes, and could swing from generosity to vindictiveness in short order with regard to both its own citizens and those of other states. This was "radical" democracy, unimpeded by the fetters of a bill of rights or judicial review. It was not disorderly or disorganized, however. The Assembly was guided by a council that arranged the business for forthcoming meetings, and everyday administration was a professional business, especially where such crucial matters as naval equipment, religious ceremonies, and public works were concerned.

It is something of a surprise that Athens survived its first thirty years as a democracy. In 499 Miletus and other cities on the coast of Asia Minor revolted against their Persian overlords. They had been conquered by Persia half a century earlier, but aside from having to pay tribute and tailor their foreign policy to that of Persia, they had enjoyed a substantial measure of self-government. What provoked the revolt is obscure, but Athens sent a fleet to assist the Milesians. It did the Milesians little good, and their revolt was snuffed out in 494; it also incurred the enmity of Persia. The first invasion of Greece took place in 490, when Darius assembled a combined naval and military force and invaded Attica. Astonishingly, when the Athenians, assisted by a substantial contingent from Plataea, confronted a much larger Persian army on the sands of

Marathon, the Persians were routed with astonishingly few casualties on the Athenian side. Although Sparta had allied with Athens to resist the "barbarian" invasion, the Spartan army was slow to arrive, and the Athenians gained the glory of the victory.

Darius's successor, Xerxes, was bent on revenge; it is said that a slave was set to remind him at every meal that the Greeks were to be subdued. In 480 Xerxes assembled an enormous army and fleet with a view to the conquest of Greece. Messengers were sent to the Greek cities demanding their submission; although many submitted, Athens and Sparta did not. The Athenians put both the messengers and their translator on trial—the latter for offenses against the Greek language—and executed them; the Spartans simply threw their visitors into a well. Diplomatic immunity was not a concept for which the ancient world had much use. The Persian army was held at the pass of Thermopylae, where the Spartans and a hoplite force from Thespis redeemed themselves by holding the pass long enough to allow the main Greek force to retreat in good order; they died to the last man. A naval battle was inconclusive, and the Athenian navy retired to the island of Salamis. The Athenian leader Themistocles persuaded the Athenians to abandon the city and retire to Salamis and await the chance of a decisive naval battle. When it came, the Persians found they had been lured into a bay where they could not maneuver and were systematically slaughtered; Xerxes, who had watched the battle, returned to Persia, leaving behind an army that was routed the following spring at the Battle of Plataea.

Over the next fifty years, Athens created an Aegean empire. What was notionally a naval and military alliance of independent equals, the Delian League, with its treasury on the sacred island of Delos, became an imperial project, with the dependent island states of the Aegean paying something closer to a simple tribute than a levy for common defense. The treasury was moved to Athens, and the city beautified at the expense of Athens's allies. The Parthenon was built between 447 and 433. At the same time, Athens became an increasingly "pure" democracy; hereditary offices held by aristocratic families were opened to lower-class citizens, leaving only some religious offices governed by the previous restrictive rules. This is not to suggest that the leading figures were anything but wellborn. Skeptical commentators on the Athenian democracy sometimes suggest that it was a disguised oligarchy, in which an elite manipulated the ordinary citizen for their own purposes. This is an exaggeration; the assembled demos did not hesitate to dismiss generals and turn against the city's leading men for whatever seemed a good enough reason or none. The institution of ostracism, which allowed the Assembly to expel anyone it chose for a period of ten years, albeit without further penalties and with the right to return at the end of the period, expressed the Assembly's intention to have no restraints on its authority. A famous tale is told of an illiterate citizen who asked Aristides, nicknamed Aristides the Just, to help him scratch the name Aristides on the potsherd, the *ostrakos*, used to cast a vote; asked what he had against Aristides, whom he had obviously never met, he replied that he was fed up hearing him called the Just. Aristides duly enhanced his reputation by filling in his name.

Athenian democracy was direct democracy, legislation by mass meeting. It has very few parallels in the modern world, where representative government is the order of the day in those societies that call themselves democracies. It was vulnerable to the obvious weaknesses of any such system, and Thucydides's *Peloponnesian War* is very sharp about the follies of the Assembly after the death of Pericles in 429. He was by no means an unbiased witness; he wrote his history after being exiled for failing to relieve the northern city of Amphipolis in 424. Nonetheless, episodes such as the destruction of Melos in 416, when all men of military age were killed, and women and children sold into slavery, remind us that democracies can behave appallingly. The execution of the generals who commanded the victorious Athenian fleet at the Battle of Arginusae but failed to recover the bodies of the Athenian dead was a piece of self-destructive wickedness by any standards. The gullibility of the Assembly is sometimes surprising; it more than once rejected the chance to end the Peloponnesian War on favorable terms, and it invariably overestimated its ability to recover from disaster. Nevertheless, its resilience and ingenuity was astonishing, and only when the Persians put their thumb on the scales by financing the Spartans and their Peloponnesian allies was Athens finally overcome. In 404 Athens surrendered; the Spartans deliberated whether to massacre the entire population of military age, but thought better of it. A short-lived collective tyranny, the Thirty Tyrants, discredited itself within months, and in 403 BCE, the democracy was restored. Modern readers of this history recall that in 399 BCE, the democracy put Socrates on trial on a charge of blasphemy, found him guilty, and sentenced him to death. Aristotle certainly remembered it and apparently said, when he left Athens as the revolt against his former student Antipater broke out in 323 BCE, that he did not wish Athens to offend against philosophy a second time.

Athens recovered surprisingly swiftly from the destruction of the Peloponnesian War, but never enjoyed the dominance over the city-states of the Aegean that it had done in the fifth century. Nor was Sparta able to capitalize on the dominance it had enjoyed at the end of the war. Shifting alliances were, as before, the order of the day, with former enemies making common cause against former allies, and Persia leaning first one way and then another as Persian interests suggested. In the course of this jockeying for advantage, Athens sacrificed the independence of the Greek cities in Asia Minor, a sad commentary on the intervention more than a century earlier that had first sparked off the Persian Wars. A new feature of the early fourth-century balance of power was the rise of Thebes; although Thebes never dominated its rivals in the way Sparta and Athens had once done, an alliance of Athens and Thebes was enough to defeat Sparta, and an alliance of Sparta and Athens enough not to defeat Thebes at the Battle of Mantinea in 362 but to leave Thebes leaderless upon the death of its great general Epaminondas, and therefore to leave Greece leaderless too.

It is not true that the Greek city-states were powerless in the face of the threat from the kingdom of Macedon, but they were certainly in no condition to meet the challenge of a well-financed invasion by a determined Philip of Macedon. The Macedonian phalanx was better armed and trained than any infantry that could be put in the field against it, and a century of warfare had in any case weakened the Greek cities, whose populations were lower in the fourth century than they had been before the outbreak of the Peloponnesian War.

Many Greek fighters had left their native cities to seek their fortunes as mercenaries with Persia or in Macedon, so the Greek cities would have had an uphill struggle even if they had found a Pericles or a Lysander to lead them. Epaminondas might have made a difference, but in the event the Battle of Chaeronea was decisive. Philip was acknowledged as hegemon, and the Greek city-state as a sovereign and independent political entity was relegated to historical memory.

It has always been remarked on that Aristotle chronicled the virtues of an essentially defunct political form when he wrote *The Politics*. It is less often remarked that in spite of asserting that the Greeks alone are fit for a properly *political* life, he draws examples of the causes of revolution and the methods of averting revolution from Persian history as well as the history of Greek city-states more narrowly. A Persian king was by Greek standards a tyrant as much as a monarch, since as often as not he would have acquired his throne by assassination rather than inheritance, and Aristotle's advice on the avoidance of stasis, or the loss of power, was available to bad rulers as well as to good.

The afterlife of Aristotle's philosophical works was complicated. He did not create a school in the same way as Plato before him and the Stoics and Epicureans after him. His extraordinary range of interests, from logic to plant breeding, from astronomy to rhetoric and the principles of rhetoric, may have baffled his successors, and his strongly empirical cast of mind, which is visible throughout his ethics and politics, may have appealed less to thinkers looking for answers to the question of how to live as a free man in conditions of political servitude, to which the Stoics had an answer and Aristotle did not. Like much of the learning of the ancient world, Aristotle's work suffered both from the accidents of warfare and from the hostility of Christian rulers to the secular philosophy of the ancient world. Whereas the library of Alexandria was first destroyed inadvertently by Julius Caesar, successor libraries were pillaged by Christian mobs, and the closure of Plato's Academy resulted from an edict of the emperor Justinian.

The recovery of Aristotle's work in the West came through a familiar route. Arab scholars preserved Greek texts and translated them, first into Arabic and then from Arabic into Latin, and they wrote numerous commentaries on his logic, metaphysics, astronomy, and much else. The first editions of his *Nicomachean Ethics* and *The Politics* readily available in the West were Latin translations from the Arabic, circulating from the twelfth century CE. One of Thomas Aquinas's many contributions to European thought was to have them translated directly from Greek texts in the middle of the thirteenth century. Aristotle's larger philosophical ideas were not easy to assimilate into a Christian framework; his belief that the universe was eternal did not mesh easily with the biblical story of creation. In politics it took an effort to turn Aristotle's liking for aristocracy into a defense of "princely rule," although philosophers from Aquinas onwards were up to the task. If Saint Paul had said that in the kingdom of God there would be neither Jew nor Gentile, slave nor free, it was clear enough that earthly kingdoms depended on a hierarchical order, to which Aristotle's notions of a natural hierarchy were wholly congenial. Only in the seventeenth century did Thomas Hobbes set out systematically to drive Aristotle's ethics and politics from the field, and his success was partial. In the physical sciences, Aristotle became hopelessly outmoded; his distinction between "natural" and "violent" motions had no place in the physics of Galileo and Newton; the idea that heavy objects fell to the ground because they were made of "sublunary" matter became the subject of mockery, as when Molière's doctor explained that sleeping potions put us to sleep because of their "dormitive power."

The same feature of Aristotle's work that ensured the (eventual) obsolescence of his physics protected his ethics and politics from the same fate. Although he was an empiricist who did his best to report the facts as he knew them, his physics was circumscribed by common sense, as well as by the teleological assumptions he shared with his teacher Plato and with the untutored common sense of everyday life. Someone who throws a baseball expects it to follow Aristotelian principles: a violent motion is imparted to it, and as a heavy object it returns to its natural place, on the ground, as the imparted motion dies out. Anyone who looks to see it travel to infinity in a uniform right line will be sorely disappointed. Of course, Galilean or Newtonian physics has ways of squaring its laws with the facts of everyday experience; it saves the appearances by introducing a great many concepts that Aristotle had no idea of. His physics "preserves the appearances" because it begins and ends with the world of ordinary human experience. But the world of ordinary human experience is precisely what ethics and politics are about. Since Aristotle was a meticulous thinker who did his level best to systematize the knowledge of his day to the degree that the subject matter allowed—as he carefully noted—what he has to say about virtue, human flourishing, the point of living in a civil society, the nature of citizenship, and a great deal else remains as interesting to us as to his listeners in the Athens of the 330s BCE or his innumerable commentators and disciples from the twelfth century onwards.

ON ARISTOTLE

Aristotle: Saving Politics
from Philosophy

❧

LIFE AND TIMES

UNLIKE PLATO, ARISTOTLE WAS embroiled in the politics of his day; indeed, he died in exile because the Athenians suspected his loyalty when they revolted against Macedonian rule in 323 BCE. He tutored Alexander the Great and also taught Antipater, the Macedonian general whom Alexander installed as regent to keep Greece in order when he left to conquer the Persian Empire in 334. The ancient historians do not suggest Aristotle was devoted to Alexander; Plutarch credits him with supplying the poison that may or may not have been the cause of Alexander's untimely death. (It was rumored that Antipater feared that Alexander had turned against him and was likely to have him executed; so Antipater preempted him.) Aristotle was born in 384 in the small town of Stagira, on the borders of Greece

and Macedon—slightly east of the modern Salonica.
He came to Athens in 367 to join Plato's Academy and
spent the next twenty years there. The forty-five years
between his arrival in Athens and his death in 322 saw
Athens's revival after the destruction of the Peloponnesian War, and then the extinction of the Greek city-
states' political independence following their defeat by
Macedonian forces, first at the Battle of Chaeronea in
338 and when the death of Alexander the Great in 323
prompted Athens to revolt, at the naval battle of
Amorgos in 322.

Aristotle's career at the Academy suffered a hiatus
after the death of Plato. He and his friend Xenocrates
left Athens when the Academy fell under the leadership
of men whom Aristotle disliked. He spent time on Les-
bos, where he was supported by the tyrant Hermias, a
former slave of great ability who had gone on to buy the
rulership of the city of Atarneus from the king of Persia. Hermias had spent time at the Academy and was
reputedly an excellent philosopher; Aristotle later married Hermias's niece, after her uncle had been tortured
and executed on the orders of the great king on suspicion of plotting to assist a Macedonian invasion of Persia. Whether Hermias brought Aristotle to the attention
of Philip of Macedon is unclear, but in 342 Aristotle
was summoned to Pella to become tutor to the young
Alexander, a position he filled until 336. It must soon

have been a part-time post, since as early as 340 Alexander was governing Macedonia in his father's absence, while two years later he commanded part of his father's army at the Battle of Chaeronea.

In 335 Aristotle returned to Athens to found his own school, the Lyceum. This was in the immediate aftermath of the second unsuccessful revolt of the Athenians against Macedonian rule. Surprisingly, neither Philip nor Alexander meted out to the Athenians the punishment meted out to Thebes, which was razed to the ground. Demosthenes, the most intransigent leader of the anti-Macedonian elements, was allowed to remain in Athens and not forced into exile. Xenocrates was now head of the Academy, but there is no suggestion that Aristotle set up in competition with his friend. There was no disloyalty in establishing his own school, and his school had a distinctive character. It was marked by an enthusiasm for empirical investigation; among other things, Aristotle founded the empirical discipline of politics by setting his students to describe and analyze 158 Greek constitutions. The "naturalism" of Aristotle's philosophy struck a balance between what we would recognize as a scientific, empirical, experimental approach to understanding the world, and a more nearly religious approach that regarded nature as the source of a beauty and order that human contrivance could not match. One result is that his political analysis is an engrossing mixture of practical wisdom and an almost Platonic attempt to show that the best state is best "by nature."

Aristotle's life in Athens after his return was not tranquil. The majority of Athenians were bitterly hostile to the hegemony of Macedon. Athenian politics until Demosthenes's death by suicide in 322 was dominated by the question of whether and how far the hegemony of Macedon could be resisted. Antipater was as unpopular as the head of an army of occupation is likely to be; and Aristotle felt himself not only a foreigner but an unwelcome one. The awkwardness was for a time reduced by Aristotle's friendship with Lycurgus, a student of both Plato and Isocrates, and now in charge of the finances of Athens and the upkeep of the city; Lycurgus was a nominal democrat and an ally of Demosthenes, but was the sort of moderate aristocratic politician praised in his *Politics*, who safeguarded the economic interests of the propertied classes and ensured they were kept friendly to the democratic constitution. Nonetheless, Aristotle's position eventually became untenable. In June 323 Alexander's unexpected death in Babylon at the age of thirty-two, whether from malaria, liver failure, or poison, provoked open revolt. Aristotle retired to Chalcis, on Euboea. He died there a year later, just as Antipater's victory at Amorgos destroyed Athenian hopes of recovering political and military independence.

ARISTOTLE'S POLITICAL PREJUDICES

Modern readers find several of Aristotle's views deeply repugnant. The two most obvious are his views on slavery and his views on the intellectual and political capacity of women.[1] Unsurprisingly, these are connected. The relation of master to inferior—of the male head of household to wife and slaves—is a basic and natural human relationship. For Aristotle the household of a man qualified to be a citizen is a family unit where slaves do the menial work: menial work unfits a man for political life; slaves and common laborers liberate the citizen for political life. The head of a household governs his family partly politically and partly not. The relation of citizen to citizen is that of equal to equal. The relation of master to slave, husband to wife, or parent to child is not one between equals, although wives are certainly free persons, whereas slaves are not.[2] Fathers exercise "royal" rule over children and "constitutional" rule over wives, but there is no suggestion that husbands and wives take turns in governing the household as citizens do the polity. We shall see how Aristotle argues for the justice of these relationships. It is worth pausing to notice two things. The first is the alarming suggestion that the acquisition of slaves is a branch of the art of war or hunting.[3] The ancient world was heavily dependent on slavery; and there were states, or pirate kingdoms, that regarded "man hunting" as a legitimate business and their own distinctive way of making a living. For villagers living within reach of their raids or for anyone forced to travel a long distance by sea, the danger of being seized and sold into slavery was very real. Aristotle suggests ways of regulating the practice of seizing captives in war and selling them into slavery, but the practice itself he does not criticize. Since he admits that many writers think slavery is unjust and contrary to nature, he certainly had the chance to do so.

The second thing to notice is that when Aristotle seeks a justification in the natural order for the existence of slavery, he appeals to the gulf in the capacity for self-government that—in his view—separates natural slaves from their masters. What he made of Hermias, the former slave, who was one of his students as well as his protector, a man to whom he dedicated a memorial and whose niece he married after her uncle's untimely death, one can only imagine. Hermias's last words were said to have been "I have done nothing unworthy of a philosopher." Along the same lines, Aristotle maintains that women are rational enough to fulfill the subordinate role in the family that he assigns to them, but have too little rational capacity to give their own independent judgment in the political arena. Women, slaves, and children belong within the well-ordered household, not in the agora or *ecclesia*. It is worth considering why readers are so often outraged that Aristotle held views that were entirely commonplace in the ancient Greek world. It is surely because so much of what he writes is strikingly down-to-earth and shows an attention to how politics is in fact conducted that is quite absent from Plato's sweeping rejection of political life in toto. Aristotle talked to many intelligent women and had every chance to change his mind; he had every opportunity to reflect on what the existence of Hermias implied for the justice of slavery. In short, modern readers might think that the remedy for Aristotle's blind spots is a more diligent application of the empirical methods he himself advocated.

TELEOLOGY: NATURE AND POLITICS

Aristotle would have been unmoved by our anachronistic advice. His conception of "nature" was not like ours, and the search for the natural order of things was not straightforwardly empirical. Hermias was transparently not a "slave by nature," but that did not mean there were no slaves by nature. Aristotle famously wrote that "it is evident that the state is a creation of nature, and that man is by nature a political animal."[4] We must, therefore, start from Aristotle's idea of nature. Aristotle is known for the doctrine of the four causes: the matter of what is to be explained; its form; the efficient cause, or how it is produced; and its final cause. The behavior of entities such as plants, animals, persons, and institutions was explained by their telos, or "end"—their goal or purpose or point. This is teleological explanation, explanation in terms of goals or purposes. The scientific revolution of the seventeenth century expelled teleological explanation from the physical sciences. Our idea of a physical cause is essentially that of the antecedent conditions that make something happen; we do not think that there is some state of affairs "proper" to physical nature, and the modern conception of nature is thus very different from Aristotle's. We use the term "natural" to describe the way things are when not affected by human contrivance—think of "natural blonde"—but Aristotle included human contrivance among the things that had their "natural" and their "unnatural" forms. A society like our own, where women have equal political rights with men, is "unnatural." "Natural" forms of life were good because they fulfilled their natural purpose. Today this Aristotelian view survives in the teaching of the Roman Catholic Church, where it is underpinned by the thought that God is the author of nature and that natural law and divine law reinforce each other. Aristotle did not think in terms of a deity who authored nature; nature itself was divine. He is therefore very exposed to the skeptical view that "natural" and "unnatural" are synonyms for "usual" and "unusual," or for "morally good" and "morally bad."

Throughout his *Politics* it is taken for granted that nature is the ground of social norms. When Aristotle asks whether there are slaves "by nature," he wants to know whether there are persons whose proper place in the world is to serve as slaves to others. If there are, it explains *both* why there is slavery *and* why it is good for (natural) slaves to be slaves. Discovering what is "natural" uncovers both the way things are and how they should be. Moreover, nature is hierarchical; everything aims at some good, and the highest things aim at the highest good. Human beings are at the top of the hierarchy of living creatures, and we must understand human behavior in the light of how we are meant to pursue the highest good. Allowances made for his prejudices, Aristotle did not simply impose a model of the good polity upon the evidence; investigating the way people do govern themselves shows how they should govern themselves.

The way to discover what nature aims to achieve is to observe what nature actually does. Nature does not always achieve the good she aims at: there are stunted trees, sickly children, unhappy marriages, and states that collapse into civil war. But we discover the standards embodied in words such as "stunted" and "diseased" by looking at what happens when things turn out well. Political science is thus a form of natural history with a strongly normative flavor. Aristotle set out the standards that explanation has to meet in his *Physics*, and they remained canonical for two millennia. The four kinds of cause—form, matter, purpose, and origin—all have their place in political analysis. The form of a state is its constitution, its matter is its citizens, its purpose is to allow us to live the best life in common, the cause of its coming into being appears from the first chapters of *Politics* to be the search for self-sufficiency; and Aristotle's discussion of revolution in later books of *Politics* is both an account of the causes of a state's ceasing to be and an account of the causes of its persistence as a going concern.

Aristotle did not share Plato's belief that all real knowledge must resemble geometry or mathematics. Plato condemned the world of sense as a poor shadow of reality. Sufficiently fine measurement will show that no equilateral triangle drawn by human hands is *perfectly* equilateral; measured sufficiently precisely, one side will be greater than another and the angles of the sides unequal. For Plato the empirical world itself was a botched copy of a transempirical reality; geometry studies perfect geometrical figures. Aristotle did not impugn the world of observation. The world is as we perceive it, though our senses can sometimes deceive us;

a man with jaundice will see things as yellow when they are not. Successful explanation should "save the appearances"; it must explain why the world we see, hear, feel, taste, and smell appears as it does. In the seventeenth century Galileo, among others, persuaded his contemporaries that the earth rotated about the sun. Although he overturned Aristotelian astronomy and physics, he professed himself a disciple of Aristotle and accepted the obligation to explain why it *looked* as though the sun moved around the earth. He rejected much of Aristotle's physics—Aristotle thought the earth was truly the center of the universe—but he accepted Aristotle's claim that a successful explanation must explain why things look the way they do.

The study of politics is a form of natural history. Thomas Hobbes loathed Aristotle's politics, and in *Leviathan* followed Plato in modeling politics on geometry; but he admired Aristotle's biology. One consequence of that "biological" style is important, not only because it was at odds with Hobbes's—and Plato's—hankering after political geometry. Aristotle claimed that political analysis should aim only "at as much precision as the subject matter permits." Political wisdom cannot aspire to the precision of geometry, and must not pretend to. Aboriculture suggests an analogy: most trees grow best in firm soil with a moderate water supply; a few thrive with their roots in mud and water. Scientists achieve deeper understanding by analyzing the differences between the trees that do the one and those that do the other. This may or may not assist the farmer, and Aristotle's writings on ethics and politics suggest that it is the farmer's needs—which is to say, in politics, the statesman's and citizen's needs—that are important. In ethics and politics we seek knowledge for the sake of action. Aristotle complains that Plato treated all knowledge as if it served the same goals, but in ethics and politics we seek the truth for the sake of knowing what to do. They are practical disciplines. We try to improve our ethical understanding by reflecting on the way we praise and blame certain actions and characters and ways of life; but we do it to live better, not to gratify curiosity.

One final aspect of this view of nature and science matters to us. Most of us today begin by thinking about the rights or the needs of individuals, and ask what sort of state has a legitimate claim on their allegiance or will best promote their welfare. That is, the individual is—to use Aristotle's terminology—"prior" to the state. Not for Aristotle. The individual is intended by nature to live and thrive in a polis, so the polis is "prior" to the individual. This has the consequence that politics is the master science or the master art, since it aims to discover the conditions under which the best state can come into being and flourish. Just as the hand is explained by its role in enabling its owner, a human person, to flourish, the qualities of citizens are explained by their role in enabling the state to flourish. An analogy might be taken from the theater. Any actor longs to play Lear or Hamlet, the first because Lear is one of the greatest tragic heroes in all drama, and the second because every skill an actor might possess is needed to display Hamlet's agonies of indecision. King Lear and Prince Hamlet are characters in Shakespeare's plays. We understand them by understanding the plays. We understand citizens by understanding the polis, and just as any actor wishes to play Hamlet or Lear, any autonomous and intelligent being would wish to play the part of a citizen in an Aristotelian polis.

ETHICS AND *THE POLITICS*

Aristotle claimed that the polis existed "by nature" because nature means us to live a good life in common. We must therefore start with his view of the good life; and because the central virtue of the polis is justice, we must see how different Aristotle's views of justice and of our motives for being just are from Plato's. In *Politics* Aristotle relies on the account of justice he gave in the *Nicomachean Ethics*. Ethics is the study of "living well." To know how to live well, we need to know the goal of human life, since knowing how well any activity has gone is a matter of knowing how far it has achieved its goal. Human life, says Aristotle, goes well when we achieve happiness, but only happiness of a certain sort, namely, happiness approved by reason. Only then are we exercising the capacities that nature intends us to exercise, and "living well." If I am a Mafia boss, and I have just murdered the entire family of a rival, men, women, and children alike, I may be happy; but I am happy because I have a vile character. No reasonable man wants to be made happy by a massacre.

Nature intends us to enjoy the happiness of a good person. This argument seems circular: we ask what the good life is and are told it is a happy life; we ask what happiness is and are told it is pleasure achieved in the right way by the right sort of person; we ask what the right sort of person is and are told it is someone who lives a life of virtue according to reason; and when we ask about the virtues, we are told that they are those habits of thought and action whose practice gives happiness to the person who has acquired the right kind of character. The argument is indeed circular but not viciously circular. To make progress, we must examine the particular virtues—reason, temperance, fidelity, courage, justice, and so on—and discover how they contribute to the good life. This is what Aristotle does. The fact that practicing the virtues can be shown to fit together in a well-conducted life gives Aristotle confidence in the framework. Once again it is worth noticing that our notions of morality and Aristotle's ideas about ethics are not quite on all fours. Many excellences that he thinks a well-found polis would encourage are not ones that we would call moral: being well-educated, having good taste, knowing how to bear ourselves in public. They are important in cementing a certain sort of social life, which is in turn important in preserving the cohesion of the polis, but they are not in the modern sense moral qualities.

Aristotle agrees with Plato that a successful polis must be built on justice, but his understanding of justice is not Plato's. The *Nicomachean Ethics* criticizes Plato for collapsing all the virtues into justice; Aristotle contrasts the justice that is one virtue among others with "justice" conceived of as virtue in general. "All-in rightness" is one thing; but justice in the usual sense is concerned with the distribution of goods and bads according to merit, giving everyone what is due. In a political context, this means the distribution of authority and power according to political virtue. A just state must have just inhabitants; states are just only if their citizens lead just lives. It would be a defect in Plato's utopia if philosophers alone could be truly just. We must therefore be able to show that an ordinary reasonable person can practice justice and will wish to do so;

but it is enough if such a person wishes to be just only under nonextraordinary conditions. *Republic* lost sight of the limits of argumentative possibility in defending the view that justice profits its practitioners *no matter what.* Plato's argument was heroic but unpersuasive because the conception of happiness to which he appealed in arguing that the just man is inevitably happier than the unjust man is too unlike ordinary happiness; Aristotle repairs the defects in Plato's case.

A just man will wish to be just as one aspect of living a good life. It is rational to be just and to acquire a just character, but there can be no guarantee that the just man will always do better than the unjust man. Nature means the just to flourish, but a given individual may be unlucky and be brought low by behaving well. A society of just persons will always do better than a society of unjust persons, and a rational man will wish to belong to such a society; but it cannot be guaranteed that every individual in such a society will thrive. Doing justice comes more easily when supported by the other virtues. A generous man will think of his family and friends and wish them to live in a just society, and that will make it easier for him to be just. Even the least-just person believes in justice to the extent of wanting everyone else to behave justly: the burglar does not wish to be burgled, nor the robber to be robbed. But a good person wants to be just for its own sake. He is made happy by being just, and being just is indispensable to the happiness he wants: he wants the trust of his friends and the respect of his peers, and these are logically connected with his being a just person, that is, the sort of person who rightly excites trust and respect.

It can be difficult to see how right Aristotle is. If we think that the deep truth about human beings is that they are self-centered "utility maximizers," it is hard to see how they can interact except by treating one another as a means to their own selfish happiness. This is the worldview of Polus, Callicles, and Thrasymachus. Aristotle did not think we are the maximizers of anything in particular. We pursue many goals, each with its own point. There is still a hierarchy of goals: a rational man subordinates the search for worldly goods to the search for excellence of character, for instance. He hopes to be honored as such, and he will care very much what others think of him; but he is not just only instrumentally. "Greed is good" is not consistent with Aristotle's view, but each genuine good has its place in a well-conducted life. There is no *general* problem of the form "Why should essentially selfish creatures care about justice, honesty, or any other virtue that benefits other people rather than themselves?" The premise of the question is false.

Human beings seek their own well-being, but not always effectively. When they fail, something has gone wrong. What is good for us is *connected* with what we want, inasmuch as the well-balanced man wants what is good for himself. But what is good for us is not *defined* as what we want, as it was by Thrasymachus; the wrong wants (think of addiction to drugs or alcohol or gambling) are disconnected from the good. Misguided wants undermine the pursuit of our good. So does simple error, as when I drink poison, believing it to be a tonic, and die when I mean to restore my health. We may make more elaborate mistakes, as when we think that harshness toward defeated enemies will make them more cooperative rather than less, or jump to conclusions, as when we succeed once in intimidating our enemies and conclude that we shall always so succeed. Other mistakes stem from deficiencies in character; a coward misreads situations as being more dangerous than they in fact are, *and* fails to see the point of courage.

POLITICAL ANALYSIS

The correct mode of political analysis seems inescapable. We should inspect whatever political regimes we can, and determine what makes for success and failure; we can distinguish corrupt governments from good governments; we can ascertain which regimes promote good political character and which the reverse; we can discover why different peoples adopt different kinds of regimes, and why what we call "politics" flourishes in some but not all societies. Aristotle sent students to discover the constitutional arrangements of Greek cities, although only *The Constitution of Athens* survives; it is itself something of a jumble and may or may not have been written by Aristotle himself rather than a student, but is fascinating nonetheless.

Politics consists of eight books, the two last very unlike their predecessors. These provide a picture of the ideal state and its educational system, a task that earlier books seemed to dismiss as a waste of time. They are also very incomplete; the final book amounts to a handful of pages devoted to the education of the young. The first six books form a well-organized argument; the first book distinguishes political associations from all others, and distinguishes their organizing principles from those of the family and the domestic household; the second discusses ideal states in theory and in practice; books 3 and 4 tackle the connected topics of forms of constitution and qualification for citizenship; and books 5 and 6 cover the connected topics of revolutionary upheaval and the construction of constitutional arrangements that will prevent or divert or defuse such upheaval.

Nonetheless, *Politics* is a sprawling work, and many

issues come up for discussion more than once. The nature of citizenship is a running theme, for instance. It is discussed in the context of forms of authority in the first book, when citizen–citizen relations are distinguished from master–slave, husband–wife, parent–children relations; that launches the repudiation of Plato's model of the polity in the second book. Qualifications for citizenship are the topic of the third and fourth books, and that subject recurs in books 5 and 6 in the context of rethinking what sorts of people should have access to political power. The pleasures of brooding on these recurrent discussions are to be had by reading *Politics* slowly. What follows here selects rather brutally, with an eye to the discussion of Plato's *Republic*, and to what others made of Aristotle in the next two millennia. My discussion does not follow Aristotle's own sequence; it initially skirts book 2, in order to end with Aristotle's attack on ideal state theory in that book, and his later ventures into that field.[5]

POLITICAL MAN

Almost at the beginning of his *Politics* Aristotle declares that man is a creature intended by nature to live in a polis. Before he does so, he makes three only slightly less famous observations. First, he claims that all associations exist for a purpose and that, as the most inclusive association, the polis exists for the most inclusive purpose. It is the ultimate form of human organization and exists to satisfy the highest goals of social life. Second, other associations need the shelter of a polis, but it requires no other association above it; it is self-sufficient and sustains a complete life for its members. Third, the correct way of governing such an association is peculiar to it; it alone should be governed "politically." Aristotle criticizes writers who conflate the authority of "statesmen"—constitutional rulers—with that of conquerors, husbands, fathers, or owners of slaves. Plato is the target. Authority in a polis is specific to it, not to be confused with authority in other relationships. A state is not a large family, and a family is not a small state. States may have begun as monarchies because they grew out of patriarchally governed clans; but if they grew out of clans, their goals are not a clan's goals. An association is to be understood in terms of its purpose rather than its origin; the purpose of the state is not that of a family or clan. The polis, he says, "grows for the sake of mere life, but it *exists* for the sake of a good life."

Aristotle has in mind the Greek city-state. Much of what he writes seems to be applicable to any state, and surprisingly often is; what he himself was concerned with was the successful functioning of the kind of state that the Athenians had created in the late sixth century, and its Greek peers. When he goes on to say that man is meant by nature to live in a polis, he means that the polis provides the environment in which human beings can best fulfill their potential and in which they can live the good life to the full. This appears on its face to contradict what he says elsewhere (and even in *Politics* itself) when claiming that the best of human lives is the philosopher's life of contemplation.[6] Aristotle has two plausible ways of resolving this tension, and his students would very likely have invoked both.

The first is to notice that few people will wish to follow the route that the philosopher follows. It may be true that *if* one has the tastes and aptitudes that philosophy demands, the life of the philosopher is uniquely fulfilling, and that nobody who has followed the life of the philosopher would wish to follow any other. Not many people have those tastes and aptitudes, and most people will find that the polis provides the environment in which they can lead the best life for them. Nor is this to say that they are "inferior" people. Their lives display virtues such as courage, justice, fidelity, honesty, and temperance; they live the best possible active rather than the best contemplative life. Nor is it a simple truth that the *vita contemplativa* is better than the *vita activa*, if it is a truth at all. The second move is to observe that the fulfillment of the philosopher is slightly odd. Aristotle claims that the man who does not need the polis is either a beast or a god; animals cannot form political societies, since they lack speech and reason, while gods are individually self-sufficient and do not need political association.[7] The philosopher aims to think God's thoughts, and if he succeeds, he also is so self-sufficient that the assessment of the success of his life escapes the usual categories. Whether this is a condition one would wish to be in, unless so irresistibly called to it as to have no choice in the matter, is a deep question not to be tackled here. It suggests yet again a tension between philosophy's search for absolutes and the political search for the modus vivendi, for ways of living together.

Aristotle devotes the first book of his *Politics* to following out the implications of this approach. Since a polis is an association of villages—he may have had in mind the demes of Athens—and a village is an association of households, he first analyzes the nature of households, with an eye to the relationship between economic and political life, always looking to differentiate the kind of authority exercised in these different spheres from political authority. Within the family, a male head governs women and children. Aristotle did not say that women were imperfect men, but he thought they were less well governed by their own reason than an educated man would be. It is therefore good for them to be governed by their husbands, and it would be bad for them to live public lives as male citizens do. A man exercises domestic authority as the head of a household, over wife, children, and slaves. As husband/father his authority is not based on force or exercised in his own narrow interests; his authority over slaves, however, is literally despotic: *despotis* means "master." The aim of his rule is to ensure that the family flourishes as a family. Aristotle bequeaths to posterity the thought that the extent and the nature of the authority that sustains human associations are determined by the functions for which the association exists, that is, by the nature of the association. Locke's analysis of the authority of government in his *Second Treatise*, published in 1690, relies on just this thought two millennia later; whether through Locke's influence or by some other route, the thought itself is enshrined in the American Constitution with its commitment to limited government, and the measuring of authority by the goals to be sought.[8]

SLAVERY

The insistence that authority follows function extends to the relationship that most troubles Aristotle's readers, slavery. Aristotle assumed that if a man (and it is only men he has in mind) was to have leisure to play a role in the political life of his society, slaves must do the manual labor that is beneath the dignity of citizens. The defenders of slavery in the antebellum American South sometimes relied on that argument, though they were more likely to draw on biblical than on philosophical inspiration, or simply to point to the miseries of "free labor" in the North, an argumentative resource not available to Aristotle. He very bleakly describes slaves as "animated tools," instruments to be set to work to achieve what their owners require of them. Greek slavery was mostly, but not always, less horrible than the plantation slavery of the southern United States and the Roman latifundia. It was easy for men, women, and children alike to end up enslaved after military defeat, with the result that many slaves were better educated than their owners, and the condition of household slaves was often tolerable. We may recall Plato's complaint that in Athens one could not distinguish slaves from citizens, or the depiction of cheerfully idle household slaves in any of Aristophanes's comedies. The same could not be said of slaves working in the silver mines at Laurium, on which Athenian prosperity depended and where miners died of overwork and lead poisoning; but the Athenians had been on the receiving end of the same treatment when they were defeated at Syracuse and set to work in the Sicilian quarries, and they neither complained on their own behalf nor softened their treatment of others. Broad humanitarianism was no more current in the classical Greek world than in the Roman world.

The view that the slave is a living implement did not imply that the owner could do with a slave anything that he might do with a plow or a spade. It was rather that *if* the relationship between master and slave is founded in nature, the disparity between the intelligence of the master and that of the slave should be of such a degree that the slave has intelligence enough only to follow instructions, and needs the master's intelligence to direct him. It would be good if masters and slaves were physically unlike as well. Nature, says Aristotle, intends slaves to have strong but unattractive bodies meant for manual labor and their masters to have attractive and athletic but less strong bodies. Sadly, nature often fails.[9] Aristotle half admits that slavery is for the most part "conventional" and that many slaves, perhaps even most, may be wrongly enslaved. He avoids undermining slavery: slavery was necessary, if politics as Aristotle understood it was to be possible. If all went well, there could even be a form of friendship between master and slave, since the master would treat the slave in ways that conduced to the slave's well-being. Unsurprisingly, when Aristotle draws up the design for an ideal state, he suggests a compromise. Greeks should not enslave Greeks, only non-Greeks, since they have servile natures, whereas Hellenes do not.[10] These remarks, which remain quite undeveloped, indicate the distance between Aristotle's casual assumption of the ethnic superiority of the Greeks over all their neighbors and modern racism, and how little intellectual pressure he was under to provide an elaborate justification of an institution that was taken for granted until the Enlightenment.

The oddity of Aristotle's views, which explains why readers so often hope that he might really be meaning to undermine the institution, is that he contradicts himself in a way he rarely does elsewhere. The thought that a slave is an animated tool suggests the slave's owner need take only the interest in the slave's welfare that he would take in the well-being of a spade. A spade needs cleaning and sharpening to be fit for digging; but nobody thinks we could be friendly with a spade. The recognition that masters and slaves often existed on good terms undermines the thought that slaves are merely tools. This is not the only contradiction; Aristotle holds, as he must, that for those who are slaves by nature, slavery is good. Yet when he discusses the ideal state, Aristotle argues that slaves should be offered the prospect of manumission, although this would not be doing them a good turn if they were suited only to slavery. Defenders of antebellum slavery were more consistent in arguing that the freed slaves would be unable to survive. If freedom would be good for them, only captives taken prisoner in a just war are rightly enslaved; and their enslavement is a punishment brought to an end by manumission. Aristotle has the same difficulties with slavery as with the authority of husband over wife. If the relationship is not arbitrary and based on brute force, the superior party must be more rational than the inferior; but not only is the inferior likely to be as rational as the superior; it is implicit in the theory that the inferior must be intelligent enough to be governed as a rational human being. If slaves and women are intellectually indistinguishable from their owners and husbands, Aristotle's framework is threatened. His mode of justification creates more problems than he can admit to. It may suggest some residual unease that he says that if, *per impossibile*, plows could act of themselves, slaves would be unnecessary.[11] It does not, of course, follow that everyone who could employ machinery in place of slaves would choose to do so; it took the American Civil War to persuade the southern states to give up their slaves. It was not obviously and indisputably irrational of the southern slave owners to make some sacrifice of economic efficiency for the sake of preserving what they saw as an aristocratic way of life.

One explanation of Aristotle's persistence in the face of difficulty lies in a different aspect of the nature of politics. When he turns to defining politics for a second time in book 7, he says that there are climatic and cultural-cum-economic reasons why only some peoples can practice politics. In the cold and barren country of the Scythians, life is so hard that it leaves no time for public debate and for the give-and-take of politics. Peoples whose energies are consumed by staying alive can practice nothing properly called politics. They live off the land, they do not form settled communities, and their tribal organization cannot sustain political life. Conversely, people who live in too hot and enervating a climate cannot sustain the vigorous debate that politics requires; they will find themselves living under a despotism. The Persians, for instance, do not govern themselves politically. They are doubly non-self-governing. They do not govern themselves, since their lives are managed by the satraps of the Persian king; and the process whereby the satraps decide how to manage the people under their control are not public processes of debate and discussion, but secret and unaccountable. Aristotle does not quite say that we cannot talk of the "politics" of the Persian monarchy; but he makes a sharp contrast between the ways events are controlled and initiated in Persia and among the Greeks. Unsurprisingly, in view of Aristotle's habit of looking for the proper course of action in the mean between two extremes, he finds the Greeks uniquely suited by nature, climate, and economy to practice politics. In Greece there is, or can be, freedom without anarchy, and order without tyranny.[12]

ECONOMIC ACTIVITY

The economic activities that permit political life to flourish can also threaten it. Aristotle considers what sort of production and consumption best sustains citizenship. As one might expect, he seeks the mean between excessive austerity and riotous moneymaking and consumerism. The Spartans were obsessed with the dangers posed by the helots whom they enslaved and kept down by murder and brutality, and with the danger of their own citizens' becoming corrupted by soft living; they kept foreign trade to a minimum and made their young men eat at military messes, so that commensality would maintain public spirit and prevent them from hankering after a comfortable private life. It worked only partially. Spartans were notoriously rapacious once away from the repressive discipline of their own city. Spartan education and militarism were not successful in internalizing the desired morality. The Spartans turned their city into a boot camp; it produced soldiers willing to die for good, bad, or indifferent reasons, but not an intelligent devotion to duty. Spartans were easy to bribe; they also lacked the cultural refinements of less militaristic states.

Aristotle shared the aims of Plato and the Spartans: to create public-spirited citizens and avoid the subversion of public spirit by private economic activity, but he hoped to achieve them by nondrastic measures. Plato admired the Spartan contempt for physical comfort; Aristotle did not. More importantly, he was skeptical of Plato's obsession with abolishing private property. He agreed that *use in common* in the context of public feasts and festivals encouraged public spirit, but he denied that production in common could be efficient. He mocked Plato's belief that the community of wives, children, and property would encourage people to transfer the sentiments ordinarily attached to "my family" and "my property" to "our" common family and property. He saw a truth that the state of much public space reinforces today; we do not think that what belongs to all of us belongs to each of us; we think it belongs to nobody, and we neglect it. For a man to have an incentive to provide for his family, he must think of it as *his* family; to have an incentive to look after his farm and crops in the most productive way, he must see them as his. Aristotle argues for private production and common use.

Even more deeply embedded is the thought that some work is intrinsically degrading and bad for the character of those who do it; and some kinds of economic activity are wrong in themselves. The basic thought is familiar. Nature tells us what we need: what food and drink, what shelter and clothing. We need enough but not too much food, drink, shelter, and comfort, as any properly brought-up person understands. We may not be able to give a very detailed account of these needs, but we do not have to. We know what work is degrading even if we cannot say exactly why; and we know that a decent person would engage in some occupations and not in others even if we cannot say exactly why. Modern economists do not ask, as Aristotle and medieval writers did, about the *proper* end or goal or purpose of economic activity; we do not talk as they did about the just price of things, though we do have a strong, if not very clear, sense that some prices and some incomes are unconscionably high or low. Trade unions have always been committed to a fair day's pay for a fair day's work, which is not so different from Aristotle's economics. Aristotle thought that our natural needs set the bounds of acceptability. We work to provide food, drink, clothing, and shelter; the aim of production is consumption. Money is therefore problematic. Official coinage was a fairly recent invention in Greek society, the oldest surviving coins dating from around 600 BCE, and was regarded with suspicion by conservative moralists such as Plato and Aristotle. The way money is "worth" things to which it bears no physical or other relationship is "unnatural." When one considers that a pair of shoes is worth or costs $175, and that this is what a hundred loaves cost or are worth, it is tempting to think that something must underpin their shared value. Whatever underpins it, it is not the fact that people will give us pieces of silver for shoes or bread; the value of money itself is what needs explanation.

Two plausible views have dominated purported explanations from that day to this. One relies on the thought that what we use requires human effort to make, catch, dig up, or find; the other relies instead on the fact that what we purchase reflects what we *want*. The first measures value by the efforts of the producers; the second measures value by the desires of the purchasers. Neither works well in all circumstances, and certainly not on its own, though they work well in combination; if I am a terrible shoemaker, my shoes will cost me much effort, but have little value in the marketplace since nobody will want to wear them. If I stumble across a diamond, it will sell for a great deal, but it will not have cost me much effort. The two thoughts together suggest that the price of anything measures its scarcity relative to the demand for it. We all need bread for survival and diamonds only when our hunger is sated; but bread is easy to produce in quantity and diamonds are not.

Aristotle began the tradition of thinking that behind the prices of goods in the marketplace there lies a true or natural value that should determine those prices. His discussion of money and usury had an enormous influence on later economic thought; most importantly, he inspired the medieval condemnation of moneylending and usury, though not of course its anti-Semitic aspects. Those flowed from the fact that Christians were supposedly prohibited from lending money at interest, and Jews were shut out of most economic activity, with the result that the Jews became moneylenders and loathed in consequence. Aristotle does not only denounce gouging or excessively high interest rates; using the biological metaphors that came so easily to him, he argued that things really useful to life were organic and that their creation and use are part of the natural cycle of production and consumption. Money is helpful when it promotes that cycle. It itself is barren, mere metal that cannot produce offspring as trees and plants do. Usury is therefore unnatural. The man who made his living by lending money at interest was setting barren metal to breed. As an unnatural way of making a living, it was to be deplored.[13]

Aristotle might be thought to be attacking the nouveaux riches. His complaints are rather more than social polemics, however. Most productive activities have a natural cycle; first we create and then we consume what we have made. Making money has no such beginning and ending. It has no natural terminus. Banking and moneymaking are solvents of social order, a point made by poets, playwrights, and social theorists ever since money was invented, and one that is made today when-

ever the excesses of operators in the financial marketplace threaten to impoverish everyone else.

Given Aristotle's views about economic activity, and
his praise of self-sufficiency, it is unsurprising that he
thought the polis is best governed by moderately well-
off men who draw their livelihood from farms on which
they themselves do not do so much work, or work of
the wrong sort, that they unfit themselves for public
life. Speaking of a regime in which farmers and the
moderately wealthy form the citizen body, he suggests
that they should have some but not too much leisure; if
they cannot spend too much time in the agora "poli-
ticking," they will have to rely on standing regulations,
that is, on the rule of law. Aristotle is the first writer to
wish for the "government of laws not of men." When
Aristotle speaks of "farmers" in that context, he means
small landowners or tenants, who owned a slave or two
with whose assistance they worked their farms;[14] at
other times he means by "farmers" those who actually
labor in the fields, and in the ideal state they would be
slaves, some owned by private individuals and some by
the state.[15] Having distinguished the domestic arts
from politics as the master art concerned to create the
conditions of a good life in common, he turns aside in
book 2 to discuss ideal states. But he has laid the foun-
dations for what most concerns him: citizenship, constitutional order, and the avoidance of stasis, and we

can follow that discussion before turning back to the ideal state.

CITIZENSHIP AND CONSTITUTION

With the ground cleared of ideal states and utopian experiments, Aristotle advances on the topics that have kept his work alive for two and a half thousand years: the nature of citizenship, the qualities of good constitutions, the causes of revolution, and prophylactics against upheaval. Their connection is that constitutions distribute power among citizens; the rules governing the gaining and use of political power are the central element of any constitution; and whether the inhabitants of a political community are content with the allocation of political rights and obligations is decisive in whether the community is stable or conflict ridden. Ways of allocating rights, obligations, and power that are least likely to provoke discontent are what we are seeking.

The subject raises questions about the connection between the qualities of the citizen as a member of a community and his qualities as an individual: loyalty, for instance, is a virtue in individuals and in the members of groups, but if the group is devoted to bad purposes, loyalty to the group is less obviously a virtue, because it will help the group achieve its (bad) goals. Criminologists suggest that there is in fact rather little honor among thieves, but our belief that there must be reflects the obvious thought that thieves who were honorable among themselves could prey on the rest of us more effectively. Whether a man can be a good citizen only by being a good man was hotly debated for the next two millennia. Among writers who drew their inspiration from ancient ideals, Machiavelli insisted that the man who is loyal to his country must often behave in ways a good man would flinch from, while Rousseau feared that Machiavelli was right and followed Plato in urging the merits of a small, simple, isolated, and uncommercial republic whose near-isolation from its neighbors would prevent the military and other entanglements that lead us into the temptation to sacrifice humanity and a wider justice to a patriotism that amounts to individual selflessness and collective selfishness. The modern nation-state has not rendered these anxieties obsolete; we are all too familiar with the fact that we know how to train young men to serve in our armed forces but do not know how to retrain them for civilian life.

Aristotle's ideas about the qualities needed by citizens reflect the assumptions of well-off Athenians about the members of different social classes as well as a hardheaded view of the way economic interests affect political behavior. Citizenship for Aristotle is not the modern world's notion, which is that of an entitlement to benefit from the protection of a particular government, and to exercise such political rights as that system confers. In most modern states, resident aliens can be expelled for misconduct; citizens cannot. Greek city-states habitually exiled their own leading citizens. Conversely, Swiss women were until recently unable to vote, but they were Swiss citizens in the modern sense of the word, since they carried Swiss passports and enjoyed the usual legal rights of inhabitants of modern states. In Aristotle's terms, they were free—not slaves—but not fully citizens. It is the right of political (but not economic) equals *to rule and be ruled in turn* that constitutes citizenship as he discusses it. Mere membership of a polity is not his central concern; nor was it to Greeks generally, living as they did in a world devoid of passports, and without the welfare arrangements that raise questions about our identities and entitlements. That is not to say that membership was unimportant; when the Athenians murdered the male inhabitants of Melos and enslaved their wives and children, membership was no light matter.

Aristotle keeps his eye on the question of who can safely be given the right to rule and be ruled in turn; and to that question his predilection for finding virtue in a mean is relevant. Since men are neither beasts nor gods, their social arrangements must suit an existence lying in a mean between the invulnerable self-sufficiency of gods and the mindless self-sufficiency of beasts. Political existence rests on a form of equality (or inequality) among men. Thinking of the constitutional arrangements that determine citizenship, he is impelled toward a familiar position. *If* there were such a difference between one man and all others as there is between a god and men or between men and animals, that man should have absolute authority.[16] There is no such difference. Conversely, if there were no difference between rich and poor, slave and free, men and women, adults and children, natives and foreigners, all could be citizens of whatever city they found themselves in. But there are important differences between them. The equality that citizenship implies is to be found in the mean position.

Aristotle did not argue that since everyone needs the protection of the laws, everyone should have the rights of (modern) citizenship. Slaves, foreigners, and women were entitled to much less than Athenian citizens, and Aristotle had no difficulties with that, even though he was himself only a resident alien in Athens. Indeed, the calmness with which he describes people in his own position is astonishing: "we call them citizens only in a qualified sense, as we might apply the term to children who are too young to be on the register, or to old men who have been relieved from state duties."[17] Nor did he suggest that human beings possess common attributes that should ground a human right to citizenship in whatever state one happened to be born in. The Stoics later argued something close to this, and it is a commonplace of liberal democratic theory, but Aristotle did not. He took it for granted that there are better and worse candidates for citizenship and that properly educated, economically independent, native-born, free men are the best. Nature meant women to be ruled by their husbands, so it would be against nature to admit women to citizenship. Men employed in repetitive manual labor where they did not exercise their own judgment were unfit to give their views on political matters. He did not argue, like later opponents of female suffrage, that women do not bear men's military burdens and therefore cannot claim the same political status; nor did he suggest that regardless of mental capacity and occupation, the fact that we are all at risk from the errors of government entitles us to a say in their activities. His test was whether a person was naturally "autonomous." Someone who was not self-governing domestically could not be part of the self-governing political community.

No Athenian believed that a Greek could be uninterested in politics. At the very least, self-defense demanded that a man keep a close eye on the holders of power; they understood what Trotsky observed twenty-five hundred years later. "You say you are not interested in politics; but politics is interested in you." The uninterest in politics and the ignorance about both politicians and political institutions displayed by British or American "citizens" of the present day would have been incomprehensible. It would also have been very surprising in such small, face-to-face communities. Within the polis politics was often class warfare; it was understood that the upper classes would try to restrict eligibility for citizenship to protect their wealth and status, and that the lower classes would try to extend their political power in self-defense. The prehistory of Athenian democracy was a long struggle to open the right to participate and hold office to those not already entitled by wealth and birth; once Athenian democracy was instituted, it remained a struggle in which the common people tried to extend their grip on the political process and the oligarchically minded tried to roll back the gains of their opponents. These struggles were sometimes conducted with a degree of savagery that no political system could readily contain; Thucydides's account of the massacres that took place all over Greece when the war between Athens and the Peloponnesian League sparked off civil wars elsewhere makes it clear that rich and poor were ready to bring in outsiders to settle local scores, and settle them violently.[18] The violence of the Thirty Tyrants during their short-lived regime was notorious, and they were violently overthrown in turn, but atrocities were commonplace all over Greece. Aristotle's obsession with political moderation is all the more compelling given the long history of immoderate behavior that constituted Greek political life. Unsurprisingly, he wants moderate persons to be citizens and institutional mechanisms to moderate conflict.

Who is to be a citizen is the obverse of the question of the best form of constitution. The nature of a constitution in Aristotle's understanding of it is very like the modern understanding: the set of rules adopted by a polis that allocates functions to institutions, and lays down who possesses the right to participate in political decision making, and how decisions affecting their polis are to be made. Aristotle felt, but resisted, the temptation to which Plato succumbed. If "the best" could rule, everyone would do well to obey them. If there was one best man, there should be a *panbasileus*, a single ruler with no check on his authority. Since by definition he would always do what was best, there could be no reason to hold him back. More plausibly, there might be a group of individuals who were "the best," and if so there should be an ideal aristocracy. Aristotle muddies the waters by assuming that "the best" would be intended by nature to form a *hereditary* ruling elite and that nature would try to ensure that the appropriate qualities would be passed down from one generation to the next. The difficulty, as the history of Athens and everywhere else attests, was that the genetic transmission of political wisdom and political flair cannot be relied on. The puzzle that obsessed Plato— why virtuous men have wicked sons—did not obsess Aristotle, but he noted the contrast between the heritability of desirable qualities that breeders could readily achieve in animals and the absence of any similar inheritance of good character in humans. To his credit, he also noticed that the "naturalness" of aristocratic rule was less obvious to nonaristocrats than to the upper classes themselves.

Aristotle came very close to the solution that would have resolved his anxieties. He had the right premises: the talent for political rule is not widely distributed, so politics is intrinsically "aristocratic"; the talent is not reliably inherited, so *hereditary* aristocracy is imperfect. Many people who do not possess political talent can recognize its presence in others; they can choose a non-hereditary aristocracy. This is modern representative government. The reason he did not suggest it is instructive. The premises were in place. Aristotle firmly believed that although the wearer of a pair of shoes may not know how to make a pair of shoes, he knows where the shoe pinches. He also went out of his way to point out that in many contexts many heads are wiser than one. He lived two millennia before the invention of modern representative government; but representative government essentially allows a democratic citizen base to choose its own rulers. It is, when it works as we hope, the device for producing an elective aristocracy that Aristotle needed in order to unite the common sense of the many with the talent of the few. James Madison and James Mill, writing within two decades of each other in the late eighteenth and early nineteenth centuries, thought that representation was the great discovery of the modern age. It allowed democratic, or more exactly popular, government on a large scale. Aristotle thought a state in which citizens did not know each other by sight was no state at all; a state was necessarily limited in size. If there were no more than a few thousand citizens, they did not need representative arrangements, and the only purpose of election would be, as at Athens, to choose the occupants of official positions. His discussion of the correct size of the citizen body implies that Athens is far too large. The idea of representative democracy did not come easily to modern thinkers; representative institutions existed centuries before they were seen as a way of creating a form of democracy, namely, "representative democracy." Rousseau proposed elective aristocracy as the best of all forms of government, but denounced the idea of representation on which the modern version of elective aristocracy rests. A few years later, Madison saw the modern argument clearly, as did Jefferson when he distinguished "pure" and "representative" forms of democracy.

ARISTOTLE'S CLASSIFICATION
OF CONSTITUTIONS

Aristocracy is in principle the best form of government: there the best men rule because they possess judgment, courage, justice, and moderation in the highest degree. They display excellence as citizens, and a constitution that places power in their hands achieves excellence as a constitution. A true aristocracy is the constitutional regime in which the few best rule in the interest of the whole. Yet experience shows that aristocracies have a regrettable habit of becoming oligarchies in which class pride, not public spirit, rules the day, and in which moderation gives way to the oppression of other social classes. To see how Aristotle resolved the difficulties as he understood them, we must turn to what he is best remembered for, the sexpartite distinction between forms of government according to the numbers who participate in them, on the one hand, and their goodness or corruption, on the other.

The three virtuous forms of government are kingship, aristocracy, and *politeia*, in which one, a few, or many persons possess ultimate power, and employ it to govern for the sake of the common good; the corrupt forms are tyranny, oligarchy, and democracy, in which one man, a few men, or the poor many govern in their own narrow interests.[19] When "democracy" became the preferred label for modern representative government, the fashion sprang up to call the bad form of popular government "ochlocracy," or mob rule; Aristotle had no such qualms. The *demos* are the "poor many," and like all Greek thinkers he assumed that the poor many would use political power in their own interest. The problem in designing a constitution is to distribute power so as to give every incentive to those who have it to use it for the common good, not in their narrow class interest. Democrats believed that poverty and the practice of mean occupations should not disqualify a man from active citizenship; Aristotle thought them doubly wrong. Poor men and practitioners of the banausic trades cannot raise their heads to contemplate the good of the whole society; as a class, the poor resent the better-off and will try to seize their wealth by whatever means they can. The "narrow democracy" or "expanded aristocracy" of the well-balanced *politeia* is the remedy. A narrow democracy would be a more restrictive version of the democracy that Cleisthenes had instituted, where the lowest social class was not yet permitted to hold most offices; conversely, an expanded aristocracy would be a system in which the requirements of birth and wealth were not as onerous as oligarchical parties wanted to institute. The thought is not complicated: too restrictive a constitution arouses resentment; too broad a constitution also does so. Somewhere in the middle ground lies the answer.

It is now clear how Aristotle connects the excellence of citizens with the excellence of the constitutional form. Although some men are undeniably superior to others, nobody is so unequivocally superior to every other man that his fellows will obey him unquestioningly. A virtuous man is more likely to be corrupted by absolute power than to become wiser and more virtuous; and untrammeled monarchical rule will turn tyrannical. Unbridled democratic government will so frighten the better-off that it will cause civil war. If it does not, it may become a collective tyranny. What is needed is what later came to be called checks and balances, and a selection process for political office that secures the service of people whose characters are adequate to the task. Nonetheless, Aristotle's perspective is not ours. Modern political discussion is imbued with a concern for individual human rights; we look to institutions to hold accountable those who wield power over their fellows, so that the rights of individuals are respected. Aristotle does not. Because he sees the world in teleological terms, he asks—as Plato did—how we can ensure that the state functions as it should. The excellence of the citizenry and the excellence of the constitution are understood in that light. Hence, of course, Aristotle's focus on the collective intelligence and collective good sense of collectives; if "the many" are not to be trusted, it remains true that many heads are better than one.

One way in which Aristotle surprises modern readers whose conception of democracy is tied to the existence of representative institutions and occasional visits to the polling booth by around half the electorate is his acceptance of the radical democratic view that *the* democratic mode of choice is the lottery.[20] Something else that surprises modern readers who reflect a little is how right he is. *If* what we wish to achieve is equal influence for all, and an equal share in the governing authority, choosing the occupants of political positions by a random procedure—a lottery—is uniquely effective. The fact that most people flinch from that conclusion suggests that—like Aristotle—they do not wish for equality of political influence above all else. They wish to secure both the benefits of aristocracy and the benefits of democracy without the defects of either. If we achieve this, we shall have created a *politeia*, the state that Aristotle claims is "on the whole best" and most likely to survive the problems that beset a political community.

THE AVOIDANCE OF STASIS

Aristotle seems to set his sights very high in arguing that the polis exists to provide the best life in common for man. But his eyes were also firmly fixed on the need to avoid revolution. The fact that *politeia* is the best practicable state is not a small matter; practicality is a central virtue in a state. Aristotle's theory of revolution, or perhaps one should say his theory of the avoidance of revolution, is interesting for innumerable reasons, of which one is that it is intrinsically highly persuasive and makes excellent sense two and a half millennia later. Aristotle's conception of revolution has two parts. It refers, on the one hand, to what he termed stasis, the situation in which political life simply could not go on any longer, and, on the other, to the bloody civil war to which this kind of breakdown could easily lead.

Stasis in the first sense is the antithesis of what every British civil servant is trained to regard as his purpose in life: "keeping the show on the road." Stasis occurs when the show is decisively off the road. But the struggle for power does not stop when matters come to a grinding halt. When an existing ruling elite, or single ruler, loses the confidence of the populace and loses the capacity to hold their attention and to coerce dissenters into obedience, it is invariably replaced by another ruler or rulers, immediately or after a period of civil war. So the other face of Aristotle's interest is in what later theorists summarized as "an unconstitutional change of constitution," not just matters coming to a grinding halt but some new ruling group seizing power. This conception of revolution embraces both what Marx and other thinkers have taught us to think of as "real" revolutions, involving insurrection, bloodshed, and the mass mobilization of the populace, and what Marx's disciples dismiss as mere coups d'état, in which no mobilization occurs and one elite is displaced by another, probably violently, but without popular involvement.

Aristotle was concerned with two situations above all, and about them he was extremely acute. The first was the tension between democratic and oligarchical factions. His interest was unsurprising, since it was this tension that marked Greek city-state politics and led to the most violent and prolonged bloodshed. He had an interesting, if schematic, view of what was at stake. His first insight was that revolution was provoked not only by a conflict of economic and social interests but also by a sense of injustice. Aristotle added the thought that two distinct conceptions of justice were at issue. The democratic conception of justice fueled the argument that men with equal political rights should be equal in their economic advantages. This suggests that revolution in democracies is essentially economic, driven by the needs of the poor or by a desire to be better-off. Unlike Marx, Aristotle did not think that the many are driven to revolt by sheer need. He thought it a brute fact about democracy that men who say to themselves that since they are equal in political status, they should be equal in everything, will turn to the elimination of economic inequality as their revolutionary project. Aristotle had no sympathy with an aspiration for economic equality. His politics is founded on the belief that nature provides for differences in intellectual and other virtues, and therefore in desert, and he did not doubt that the better-off were generally entitled to their wealth and social position. The point was to meet everyone's aspirations sufficiently to preserve political stability.

If the democratic conception of justice might lead to an economic revolution among people who have the same political rights as their economic superiors, an oligarchical revolution proceeds in exactly the opposite way. The oligarchical notion of justice was that men who were unequal in wealth ought to be unequal in everything, that they should remove the political rights of the many and monopolize power as well as wealth. The history of Athens would have seemed to Aristotle sufficient evidence for this thought; but he could have drawn on innumerable other examples. The Peloponnesian War had been marked by savage struggles between oligarchs and democrats all over Greece and throughout the Aegean, and city-states were torn apart as oligarchs in one city aided their counterparts in another and democrats came to the aid of democrats.

Aristotle's delicacy of touch comes out in his recipes for holding off the evils of stasis. Even relatively bad states can profit from the intelligent application of the rules of self-preservation. Aristotle was happy even to advise tyrannical regimes on preserving their power. His advice has been echoed through the ages, and makes a great deal of sense. It is simple enough, though hard to follow. Since what disables a tyrant is either the simple illegitimacy of his rule or the wickedness of his behavior, and the first of these is by definition irremediable, he must adopt a double strategy; on the one hand, he must keep his opponents divided, so that they do not unite against him, and on the other, try to behave as a decent monarch who had come to power by constitutional means would do: moderately and virtuously. Pre-echoing Machiavelli and other advisers to princes ever since, Aristotle advises against undue greed and self-indulgence; the rationally self-interested tyrant, to employ the idiom of a much later day, will sacrifice the pleasures of the flesh and the satisfaction of personal grudges, to protect his hold on power. In particular, he should be careful to eschew sexual advances to the wives and children of upper-class men. It is one thing to deprive others of their rightful share in the government of their society, quite another to affront their family pride and their honor by assaulting the chastity of their wives and daughters. The same advice evidently applies to seizing their property. The tyrant whom Polus imagines in *Gorgias* would be short-lived.

The advice suggests Aristotle's concern to analyze how a state could function smoothly rather than to moralize from the sidelines about the wickedness of tyrants. The modern tendency to restrict the term "tyrant" to murderous dictators in the mold of Idi Amin makes Aristotle's willingness to give advice to tyrants on how to preserve their position seem more shocking than it is. Aristotle's patron and uncle-in-law, Hermias, was a good man but technically a tyrant. Not everyone was as unlucky as Plato in Sicily. Moreover, in Aristotle's day there was no such disparity between rulers and ruled in their access to murderous military power as there is today. Tyrants were uneasier then than now and had to watch their step in a way their modern successors do not have to, as long as they can preserve the allegiance of their armed forces.

Given his advice to tyrants, it is easy to guess that Aristotle advises other regimes to look to their strengths and avoid their weaknesses. Democracies are in danger of provoking revolution if they add to the distress caused to the traditional ruling elite when it was forced to yield power to the poor; so attempts to create an equality of wealth as well as an equality of power should be eschewed. The temptation to load all the burdens of public life onto the backs of the well-off should be resisted. Moreover, the better-off ought to be allowed a proper place in the political system; the more democracy counterbalances itself with the characteristics of aristocracy, the safer and longer lasting the regime will be. The converse holds good for oligarchies; they must strengthen those features that will make them less repugnant to democrats, and should endeavor to avoid the risk of a revolution in which the poor many revolt against being reduced to near-slavery.

In offering this advice, Aristotle began a tradition of empirically minded constitutional theorizing often described as the theory of the mixed constitution; his place in that tradition, however, is not easy to characterize. Commonly, theories of the mixed constitution set out to provide a recipe for achieving the advantages of monarchy, aristocracy, and democracy within one "mixed" constitution. Two centuries later, Polybius praised the Romans for adopting the recipe. More recently, much self-congratulatory thinking about British politics has pointed to the mixture of Crown, Lords, and Commons as such a mixed system, matched by American self-congratulation on the subject of the virtues of a separation of powers and the ability of executive, legislative, and judiciary to check and balance one another. Aristotle was interested in something different. His recipe for a stable governmental system relied on matching political power and economic interest, and it anticipated the findings of twentieth-century political science. A political system that gives political power to the majority of the citizens so long as they also possess the majority of society's wealth is uniquely likely to be stable. This requires what sociologists called a "lozenge-shaped" distribution of wealth; if there are few very poor people, few very rich people, and a substantial majority of "comfortably off" people in a society, the middling sort with much to lose will outvote the poor and not ally with them to expropriate the rich; conversely, they will be sufficiently numerous to deter the rich from trying to encroach upon the rights and wealth of their inferiors. American political sociologists explained the resilience of American democracy by noting the United States' achievement of this happy condition after World War II. This is not an account of a mixed constitution in the sense of a regime that combines elements of monarchy, aristocracy, and democracy, but an argument about the economic basis of political stability. Nonetheless, both it and the genuinely mixed regime reflect Aristotle's search for a mean between extremes, as he acknowledges. He admits that commentators praise the mixed regime; it certainly benefits from being a mixture, just as bronze is stronger than the metals of which it is an alloy, but Aristotle's interest is really in what to do if we cannot simply rely on "the best men."

One-man rule degenerates too easily into tyranny, and democracy into mob rule; dictators are proud and prone to run amok, and the poor are ignorant and prone to be misled by demagogues. One difficulty Aristotle faced in giving unequivocal assent to the virtues of the mixed regime in the strict sense was that the system was made famous by Sparta; and Sparta failed in the task of encouraging the widest range of excellences among its citizens because it was devoted to one excellence only, military prowess. Aristotle relies instead on the good sense and steadiness of the middling sort, and his *politeia* allows the middling sort to exercise a preponderance of power that should ensure that things never get out of hand. This is why the distribution of wealth and income must support the distribution of political power. In 1961 Seymour Martin Lipset published a justly famous account of the conditions for stable liberal democratic government, freely acknowledging his debts to Aristotle and entitling the volume in which his argument appeared *Political Man*.[21] Dante's description of Aristotle as "the master of the wise" holds up very well six centuries after Dante.

A modern treatment of the subject would emphasize that if the middle class outnumbers the poor, as it is said to do in most prosperous modern economies, there is little advantage to be had in reducing the poor to beggary; even if the poor have some resources to exploit, the payoff for each member of the middle classes is too small to provide an incentive for misbehavior. Aristotle does not argue in those terms; he focuses rather on the effects of occupying a middle-class position on the character of middle-class people. The moderate social and economic condition of their lives would create a corresponding moderation in their desires; they would not wish to tear down their betters or to oppress their inferiors. Once again, we have to remember the principle that in all subjects we should aim only at as much precision as the subject affords. Aristotle's views do not apply to all times and all places, or to all sorts of economies. The middle class in modern liberal democracies is not exactly the middle ranks of Greek society, nor should we extrapolate from a small, poor agricultural economy to a modern industrial economy with an elaborate and extensive public sector. The panic-stricken middle class that has been accused of bringing Hitler to power, described by Marxists as the *wildgewordene Kleinbürger*, is not what Aristotle had in mind. While we may admire the ingenuity of Aristotle's analysis, we cannot simply "apply" it to ourselves. Nonetheless, it remains astonishingly suggestive.

IDEAL STATES

Aristotle's genius was for showing the ways in which we might construct the "best practicable state." This was not *mere* practicality; the goals of political life are not wholly mundane. The polity comes into existence for the sake of mere life, but it continues to exist for the sake of the good life. The good life is richly characterized, involving as it does the pursuit of justice, the expansion of the human capacities used in political debate, and the development of all the public and private virtues that a successful state can shelter—military courage, marital fidelity, devotion to the physical and psychological welfare of our children, and so on indefinitely. For this project to be successful, the state must practice what Aristotle regarded as politics in its essence. This essence is the bringing together of a diversity of people with a diversity of interests—to the degree that a community of Greeks from the fourth century BCE is not anachronistically described in such terms.

One of Aristotle's most famous distinctions was the one he drew between the mere gregariousness of bees and cattle and the *political* character of human beings. Recent evolutionary theory suggests that he may have underestimated the complexity of the social lives of bees and ants, but the distinction he had in mind holds up well enough. Gregarious animals come together without speech; their need for one another brooks no discussion. People unite in a political society only by agreement on the *justice* of the terms on which they do so. This agreement invites a lot of discussion. This is a thought that Hobbes later twisted to his own ends, claiming, quite falsely, that Aristotle had described ants and bees as naturally political, and going on to argue that humans were not naturally political precisely because they had to establish political communities by agreement on principles of justice.[22] The power of Aristotle's argument is perhaps attested by Hobbes's need to misrepresent it while stealing it for his own purposes.

The fact that politics achieves unity out of a plurality of interests and beliefs without suppressing them is the moral that Aristotle draws from his glancing discussion of Plato's *Laws* and *Republic* in book 2. The book discusses the theory and practice of ideal communities, but Plato's picture of utopia receives the most attention. If it is really true that Aristotle had worked with Plato on the writing of *Laws* when he was a student in the Academy, it would explain the similarities between the ideal state that Aristotle sets out in books 7 and 8 and the polity of *Laws*. In book 2, however, Aristotle criticizes *Republic* and *Laws* very severely. Plato, says Aristotle, was obsessed with disunity. This was not unreasonable. Athens was always on the verge of civil war; social class was set against social class; and the city's self-esteem was fueled by constant wars with its neighbors. The attractions of social cohesion, and of a society that did not keep peace at home by waging war abroad, were obvious. Still, Plato's attempt to secure peace by making the polis an archetype of a unitary order is a mistake.

It is a mistake because it turns a city into something other than a city. It is of the essence of the city that it is a compound of parts that have to be kept in a constantly changing but orderly relation to one another. Aristotle was the first critic to level against Plato the charge that has a particular resonance today as a criticism both of a certain sort of overly rationalistic politics and of the totalitarian state to which that kind of politics can lead. Plato does not provide for a better politics but for a society with no politics. He has purified politics to death. Nonetheless, Aristotle felt the attraction of this mode of thinking. At the heart of the attraction was the impulse to self-sufficiency. The centrality of self-sufficiency to Aristotle's analysis is evident. The polis is logically prior to the individual as being the more self-sufficient of the two; individuals must live in a polis because they are not individually self-sufficient. This is not merely a matter of physical survival; it is a moral matter as well. Without mutual discipline, men become worse than animals. The being with no need of a city is either a God or a beast. The temptation is to think that the more complete the unity of the city, the greater the degree of self-sufficiency, and the greater its immunity to the ravages of time and conflict.

Both the larger claim that Plato abolishes politics by overemphasizing unity and Aristotle's particular criticisms of Plato's work are well taken. We have already seen his defense of the family, his acceptance of the need for private property, and his skepticism whether Plato's abolition of family life for the guardians would mean their loyalties were transferred to the city. No doubt, some sorts of moneymaking are unnatural, and property for use is more natural than property for exchange and acquisition, but that does not impugn the desirability of private property as such. Aristotle approved of the Spartan tradition of making their young men dine in common messes, without thinking that it implied the end of private ownership or that Spartan austerity was good for us. Aristotle finally produced a devastating objection to Plato's belief that the society described in *Republic* would be happy. Plato had said that in spite of the deprivation of property, family, and private life, the guardians would be happy serving the polis; but he backed away from that claim and argued that the *city* would be happy—implicitly admitting that many of the citizens would not be. To which Aristotle replied that happiness was not the sort of thing that could exist in the whole without existing in the parts. If the citizens were not happy, the polis was unhappy.

Yet Aristotle ends his *Politics* by setting up his own version of an ideal state. Exactly what is happening in books 7 and 8 is obscure, in the sense that, even more than elsewhere in *Politics*, Aristotle recurs to themes tackled elsewhere, in ways that threaten the consistency of the work. The dismissive treatment of the construction of utopias in book 2 casts doubt on whether the project of books 7 and 8 makes much sense. That book's insistence that politics is the art of constructing a setting for the good life against the background of difficulties that can be controlled but never eliminated suggests that constructing ideal states is a dubious undertaking, suffering the problems suggested by the famous joke against the economist on a desert island who responds to the absence of a can opener with which to open the canned food washed up with himself and his companions with the sentence "Let x be a can opener."

Nonetheless, the last two books of *Politics* have an interest as revealing what Aristotle thought perfection would look like. Like Plato, Aristotle turns a central problem of politics on its head; abandoning the question "Given the frailties and imperfections of human character, how does a statesman preserve order and pursue the common good?" to answer the question "How does a statesman ensure that the citizens are of good and amenable character?" Aristotle produces the town planner's ideal state. The ideal polis will have no more than ten thousand citizens, so that all citizens can know one another, and in this context Aristotle makes his famous observation that a state can be neither too little nor too large, and rashly appeals to the obviousness of the fact that a ship cannot be five feet long or five hundred. Readers may wonder what we should call supertankers or the Chinese state. The citizens will be supported by an agricultural economy in which slaves will supply the workers needed for the farms, and the citizens will be fed at common tables. The detail into which Aristotle goes when discussing where the common tables should be established and especially where the common tables sponsored by the officials of the city should be located is surprising in itself and an indicator of the grip that Sparta exercised on his imagination as well as Plato's. It may also reflect his friendship with Lycurgus, who was responsible for the organization of festivals and the like.

More importantly, it reminds us that Aristotle's emphasis on the plurality of legitimate interests that politics exists to reconcile is not the ancestor of the social, moral, and religious pluralism of modern political liberalism. For although Aristotle acknowledges that different elements in a community will have strong views about the justice of their share of the benefits and burdens of social and political life, he does not acknowledge that they might legitimately have different and irreconcilable views about the nature of justice or the nature of the good life. The perspective is authoritarian. One aspect of this is Aristotle's uninterest in any such concept as that of privacy. For Aristotle, it is perfectly proper for the state to regulate the sexual and family lives of its citizens; he sets down strict rules governing the ages at which men and women should have children, and provides for compulsory abortion where women become pregnant in a way that might imperil population policy or produce unhealthy children. In the process, he begins a long history of controversy by suggesting that when miscarriages are induced, it should be before the fetus has life and sense, which he puts at the time of quickening.

In short, Aristotle's conceptions of a free society, political freedom, and the free man are not wholly foreign to us, but they are not ours. One can see this vividly in his fragmentary remarks about education at the very end of *Politics*. Aristotle is perhaps the first author of a theory of liberal education, which is to say, an account of the value of an education devoted to knowing things that are worth knowing for their own sake, and calculated to make the young man who learns them a gentleman. The definition of a liberal education as a *gentleman*'s education persisted into modern times; when

Cardinal Newman wrote *The Idea of a University* in the middle of the nineteenth century, he declared that the object of a university was to turn out "gentlemen." Conversely, Locke's more utilitarian and vocational account of education had made an impact a century and a half earlier precisely because it subverted the older Aristotelian picture. But "liberal" in this context has nothing to do with political liberalism. It means "nonvocational" or "suited to a free spirit," and its social connotations are unabashedly aristocratic.

A piece of advice that strikes oddly on the modern ear is that well-bred young people ought to learn to play a musical instrument but not with such skill that they might be mistaken for professional musicians. This was not simple snobbery, or a matter of urging that a violinist of good family ensure he was not mistaken for Menuhin or Heifetz. Professional musicians were in demand in places of ill repute, hired in for parties at which prostitutes provided the entertainment. Today we would not expect a stag party to hire both strippers and a string quartet. Nonetheless, Aristotle's enthusiasm for the preservation of social distinction and his emphasis on the social position of the "high-souled" man remind us that even in his favored *politeia*, with as many respectable and steady men of the middle class admitted to political participation as is possible, Aristotle hankered after the rule of true, that is, *natural* aristocrats. If that attitude is not unknown two and a half millennia later, his unconcern with those left out of this vision of the world—women, ordinary working people, foreigners, slaves—is happily rather less common. But we do not see much sympathy for ordinary lives and ordinary happiness for many centuries more.

NOTES

1. Aristotle, *The Politics and The Constitution of Athens*, ed. Stephen Everson, trans. Jonathan Barnes (Cambridge: Cambridge University Press, 1996) (1.4–7, slaves; 12–13, women), pp. 12–15, 27–30.
2. Ibid. (1.12), p. 27.
3. Ibid. (1.7), p. 19.
4. Ibid. (1.2), p. 13.
5. Though some commentators think the conventional ordering of *Politics* is anyway not what Aristotle originally intended.
6. Aristotle, *Politics* (7.2), pp. 168–69.
7. Ibid. (1.2), p. 8.
8. John Locke, *Second Treatise* (sections 89–90), in *Two Treatises of Government*, ed. Peter Laslett (Cambridge: Cambridge University Press, 1998), pp. 325–26.
9. Aristotle, *Politics* (1.5), p. 17.
10. Ibid. (7.2), p. 181.
11. Ibid. (1.4), p. 15.

12. Ibid. (7.7), p. 175.

13. Ibid. (1.10), p. 25.

14. Ibid. (4.6), p. 100.

15. Ibid. (7.10), pp. 180–81.

16. Ibid. (3.13), pp. 80–83.

17. Ibid. (3.1), p. 62.

18. Thucydides, *The Peloponnesian War*, ed. and trans. Steven Lattimore (Indianapolis: Hackett, 1998), pp. 164–72.

19. Aristotle, *Politics* (3.7), p. 71.

20. Ibid. (4.9), pp. 104–5.

21. Seymour Martin Lipset, *Political Man: The Social Bases of Politics* (Garden City, N.Y.: Doubleday, 1960), foreword, pp. 7–10.

22. Thomas Hobbes, *Leviathan*, ed. Richard Tuck (Cambridge: Cambridge University Press, 1991), p. 119.

Selections

❧

A NOTE ON THE SELECTIONS

Nobody knows quite how closely the modern text of *Politics* mirrors what a young man might have read in the Lyceum. The layout is, to say the least, somewhat awkward. Book 2 discusses ideal states and appears to conclude that building ideal states is a waste of effort; we should work inductively, extrapolating from best practice to improve existing political systems. But books 7 and 8 set out to describe the ideal state. Throughout *Politics*, Aristotle takes two or more bites at the same topic, sometimes referring to other discussions and often not. Broadly, book 1 distinguishes political rule from other sorts of authority and politics from household management; book 2 discusses ideal states and is especially sharp with Plato's advocacy in *Republic* of a community of wives and property; book 3 discusses citizenship and leads

naturally into book 4, which further discusses the varieties of political systems; book 5 is an extended discussion
of stasis or revolution; book 6 is a rather miscellaneous
discussion of public office and eligibility for office; books
7 and 8 end with an unfinished discussion of the ideal
state, which is rich in ideas about the good life and how
it is to be lived, but may puzzle modern readers with its
long and ambivalent discussion of musical education. As
throughout *Politics*, the ghost of Plato's discussion of education in *Republic* seems to haunt the text.

NICOMACHEAN ETHICS
Translated by J. E. C. Welldon

BOOK I
Chapter I

Every art and every scientific inquiry, and similarly
every action and purpose, may be said to aim at some
good. Hence the good has been well defined as that at
which all things aim. But it is clear that there is a difference in the ends; for the ends are sometimes activities,
and sometimes results beyond the mere activities. Also,
where there are certain ends beyond the actions, the
results are naturally superior to the activities.

As there are various actions, arts, and sciences, it
follows that the ends are also various. Thus health is

the end of medicine, a vessel of shipbuilding, victory of strategy, and wealth of domestic economy. It often happens that there are a number of such arts or sciences which fall under a single faculty, as the art of making bridles, and all such other arts as make the instruments of horsemanship, under horsemanship, and this again as well as every military action under strategy, and in the same way other arts or sciences under other faculties. But in all these cases the ends of the architectonic arts or sciences, whatever they may be, are more desirable than those of the subordinate arts or sciences, as it is for the sake of the former that the latter are themselves sought after. It makes no difference to the argument whether the activities themselves are the ends of the actions, or something else beyond the activities as in the above mentioned sciences.

If it is true that in the sphere of action there is an end which we wish for its own sake, and for the sake of which we wish everything else, and that we do not desire all things for the sake of something else (for, if that is so, the process will go on *ad infinitum*, and our desire will be idle and futile) it is clear that this will be the good or the supreme good. Does it not follow then that the knowledge of this knowing supreme good is of great importance for the conduct of life, and that, *if we know it*, we shall be like archers who have a mark at which to aim, we shall have a better chance of attaining what we want? But, if this is the case, we must endeavor to comprehend, at least in outline, its nature, and the science or faculty to which it belongs.

It would seem that this is the most authoritative or architectonic science or faculty, and such is evidently the political; for it is the political science or faculty which determines what sciences are necessary states, and what kind of sciences should be learnt, and how far they should be learnt by particular people. We perceive too that the faculties which are held in the highest esteem, e.g. strategy, domestic economy, and rhetoric, are subordinate to it. But as it makes use of the other practical sciences, and also legislates upon the things to be done and the things to be left undone, it follows that its end will comprehend the ends of all the other sciences, and will therefore be the true good of mankind. For although the good of an individual is identical with the good of a state, yet the good of the state, whether in attainment or in preservation, is evidently greater and more perfect. For while in an individual by himself it is something to be thankful for, it is nobler and more divine in a nation or state.

These then are the objects at which the present inquiry aims, and it is in a sense a political inquiry. But our statement of the case will be adequate, if it be made with all such clearness as the subject-matter admits; for it would be as wrong to expect the same degree of accuracy in all reasonings as in all manufactures. Things noble and just, which are the subjects of investigation in political science, exhibit so great a diversity and uncertainty that they are sometimes thought to have only a conventional, and not a natural, existence. There is the same sort of uncertainty in regard to good things, as it often happens that injuries result from them; thus there have been cases in which people were ruined by wealth, or again by courage. As our subjects then and our premisses are of this nature, we must be content to indicate the truth roughly and in outline; and as our subjects and premisses are true generally *but not universally*, we must be content to arrive at conclusions which are only generally true. It is right to receive the particular statements which are made in the same spirit; for an educated person will expect accuracy in each subject only so far as the nature of the subject allows; he might as well accept probable reasoning from a mathematician as require demonstrative proofs from a rhetorician. But everybody is competent to judge the subjects which he understands, and is a good judge of them. It follows that in particular subjects it is a person of *special* education, and in general a person of universal education, who is a good judge. Hence the young are not proper students of political science, as they have no experience of the actions of life which form the premisses and subjects of the reasonings. Also it may be added that from their tendency to follow their emotions they will not study the subject to any purpose or profit, as its end is not knowledge but action. It makes no difference whether a person is young in years or youthful in character; for the defect *of which I speak* is not one of time but is due to the emotional character of his life and pursuits. Knowledge is as useless to such a person as it is to an intemperate person. But where the desires and actions of people are regulated by reason the knowledge of these subjects will be extremely valuable.

POLITICS

Translated by Benjamin Jowett

BOOK I

Chapter I

Every state is a community of some kind, and every community is established with a view to some good; for mankind always act in order to obtain that which they think good. But, if all communities aim at some good, the state or political community, which is the highest of all, and which embraces all the rest, aims at good in a greater degree than any other, and at the highest good.

Some people think that the qualifications of a statesman, king, householder, and master are the same, and that they differ, not in kind, but only in the number of their subjects. For example, the ruler over a few is called a master; over more, the manager of a household;

over a still larger number, a statesman or king, as if there were no difference between a great household and a small state. The distinction which is made between the king and the statesman is as follows: When the government is personal, the ruler is a king; when, according to the rules of the political science, the citizens rule and are ruled in turn, then he is called a statesman.

But all this is a mistake; for governments differ in kind, as will be evident to any one who considers the matter according to the method which has hitherto guided us. As in other departments of science, so in politics, the compound should always be resolved into the simple elements or least parts of the whole. We must therefore look at the elements of which the state is composed, in order that we may see in what the different kinds of rule differ from one another, and whether any scientific result can be attained about each one of them.

Chapter 2

He who thus considers things in their first growth and origin, whether a state or anything else, will obtain the clearest view of them. In the first place there must be a union of those who cannot exist without each other; namely, of male and female, that the race may continue (and this is a union which is formed, not of deliberate purpose, but because, in common with other animals and with plants, mankind have a natural desire to leave behind them an image of them-selves), and of natural ruler and subject, that both may be preserved. For that which can foresee by the exer-cise of mind is by nature intended to be lord and mas-ter, and that which can with its body give effect to such foresight is a subject, and by nature a slave; hence master and slave have the same interest. Now nature has distinguished between the female and the slave. For she is not niggardly, like the smith who fashions the Delphian knife for many uses; she makes each thing for a single use, and every instrument is best made when intended for one and not for many uses. But among barbarians no distinction is made between women and slaves, because there is no natural ruler among them: they are a community of slaves, male and female. Wherefore the poets say,

"It is meet that Hellenes should rule over barbarians";

as if they thought that the barbarian and the slave were by nature one.

Out of these two relationships between man and woman, master and slave, the first thing to arise is the family, and Hesiod is right when he says,

"First house and wife and an ox for the plough,"

for the ox is the poor man's slave. The family is the association established by nature for the supply of men's everyday wants, and the members of it are called by Charondas "companions of the cupboard," and by Epimenides the Cretan, "companions of the manger." But when several families are united, and the association aims at something more than the supply of daily needs, the first society to be formed is the village. And the most natural form of the village appears to be that of a colony from the family, composed of the children and grandchildren, who are said to be suckled "with the same milk." And this is the reason why Hellenic states were originally governed by kings; because the Hellenes were under royal rule before they came together, as the barbarians still are. Every family is ruled by the eldest, and therefore in the colonies of the family the kingly form of government prevailed because they were of the same blood. As Homer says:

> "Each one gives law to his children and to his wives."

For they lived dispersedly, as was the manner in ancient times. Wherefore men say that the Gods have a king, because they themselves either are or were in ancient times under the rule of a king. For they imagine, not only the forms of the Gods, but their ways of life to be like their own.

When several villages are united in a single complete community, large enough to be nearly or quite self-sufficing, the state comes into existence, originating in the bare needs of life, and continuing in existence for the sake of a good life. And therefore, if the earlier forms of society are natural, so is the state, for it is the end of them, and the nature of a thing is its end. For what each thing is when fully developed, we call its nature, whether we are speaking of a man, a horse, or a family. Besides, the final cause and end of a thing is the best, and to be self-sufficing is the end and the best.

Hence it is evident that the state is a creation of nature, and that man is by nature a political animal. And he who by nature and not by mere accident is without a state, is either a bad man or above humanity; he is like the

"Tribeless, lawless, hearthless one,"

whom Homer denounces—the natural outcast is forthwith a lover of war; he may be compared to an isolated piece at draughts.

Now, that man is more of a political animal than bees or any other gregarious animals is evident. Nature, as we often say, makes nothing in vain, and man is the only animal whom she has endowed with the gift of speech. And whereas mere voice is but an indication of pleasure or pain, and is therefore found in other animals (for their nature attains to the perception of pleasure and pain and the intimation of them to one another, and no further), the power of speech is intended to set forth the expedient and inexpedient, and therefore likewise the just and the unjust. And it is a characteristic of man that he alone has any sense of good and evil, of just and unjust, and the like, and the association of living beings who have this sense makes a family and a state.

Further, the state is by nature clearly prior to the family and to the individual, since the whole is of necessity prior to the part; for example, if the whole body be destroyed, there will be no foot or hand, except in an equivocal sense, as we might speak of a stone hand; for when destroyed the hand will be no better than that. But things are defined by their working and power; and we ought not to say that they are the same when they no longer have their proper quality, but only that they have the same name. The proof that the state is a creation of nature and prior to the individual is that the individual, when isolated, is not self-sufficing; and therefore he is like a part in relation to the whole. But he who is unable to live in society, or who has no need because he is sufficient for himself, must be either a beast or a god: he is no part of a state. A social instinct is implanted in all men by nature, and yet he who first founded the state was the greatest of benefactors. For man, when perfected, is the best of animals, but, when separated from law and justice, he is the worst of all; since armed injustice is the more dangerous, and he is equipped at birth with arms, meant to be used by intelligence and virtue, which he may use for the worst ends. Wherefore, if he have not virtue, he is the most unholy and the most savage of animals, and the most full of lust and gluttony. But justice is the bond of men in states, for the administration of justice, which is the determination of what is just, is the principle of order in political society.

Chapter 3

Seeing then that the state is made up of households, before speaking of the state we must speak of the management of the household. The parts of household management correspond to the persons who compose the household, and a complete household consists of slaves and freemen. Now we should begin by examining everything in its fewest possible elements; and the first and fewest possible parts of a family are master and slave, husband and wife, father and children. We have therefore to consider what each of these three relations is and ought to be:—I mean the relation of master and servant, the marriage relation (the conjunction of man and wife has no name of its own), and thirdly, the procreative relation (this also has no proper name). And there is another element of a household, the so-called art of getting wealth, which, according to some, is identical with household management, according to others, a principal part of it; the nature of this art will also have to be considered by us.

Let us first speak of master and slave, looking to the needs of practical life and also seeking to attain some better theory of their relation than exists at present. For some are of opinion that the rule of a master is a science, and that the management of a household, and the mastership of slaves, and the political and royal rule, as I was saying at the outset, are all the same. Others affirm that the rule of a master over slaves is contrary to nature, and that the distinction between slave and freeman exists by law only, and not by nature; and being an interference with nature is therefore unjust.

Chapter 4

Property is a part of the household, and the art of acquiring property is a part of the art of managing the household; for no man can live well, or indeed live at all, unless he be provided with necessaries. And as in the arts which have a definite sphere the workers must have their own proper instruments for the accomplishment of their work, so it is in the management of a household. Now instruments are of various sorts; some are living, others lifeless; in the rudder, the pilot of a ship has a lifeless, in the look-out man, a living instrument; for in the arts the servant is a kind of instrument. Thus, too, a possession is an instrument for maintaining life. And so, in the arrangement of the family, a slave is a living possession, and property a number of such instruments; and the servant is himself an instrument which takes precedence of all other instruments. For if every instrument could accomplish its own work, obeying or anticipating the will of others, like the statues of Daedalus, or the tripods of Hephaestus, which, says the poet,

> "of their own accord entered the assembly of the Gods";

if, in like manner, the shuttle would weave and the plectrum touch the lyre without a hand to guide them, chief workmen would not want servants, nor masters slaves. Here, however, another distinction must be drawn; the instruments commonly so called are instruments of production, whilst a possession is an instrument of action. The shuttle, for example, is not only of use; but something else is made by it, whereas of a garment or of a bed there is only the use. Further, as production and action are different in kind, and both require instruments, the instruments which they employ must likewise differ in kind. But life is action and not production, and therefore the slave is the minister of action. Again, a possession is spoken of as a part is spoken of; for the part is not only a part of something else, but wholly belongs to it; and this is also true of a possession. The master is only the master of the slave; he does not belong to him, whereas the slave is not only the slave of his master, but wholly belongs to him. Hence we see what is the nature and office of a slave; he who is by nature not his own but another's man, is by nature a slave; and he may be said to be another's man who, being a human being, is also a possession. And a possession may be defined as an instrument of action, separable from the possessor.

Chapter 5

But is there any one thus intended by nature to be a slave, and for whom such a condition is expedient and right, or rather is not all slavery a violation of nature?

There is no difficulty in answering this question, on grounds both of reason and of fact. For that some should rule and others be ruled is a thing not only necessary, but expedient; from the hour of their birth, some are marked out for subjection, others for rule.

And there are many kinds both of rulers and subjects (and that rule is the better which is exercised over better subjects—for example, to rule over men is better than to rule over wild beasts; for the work is better which is executed by better workmen, and where one man rules and another is ruled, they may be said to have a work); for in all things which form a composite whole and which are made up of parts, whether continuous or discrete, a distinction between the ruling and the subject element comes to fight. Such a duality exists in living creatures, but not in them only; it originates in the constitution of the universe; even in things which have no life there is a ruling principle, as in a musical mode. But we are wandering from the subject. We will therefore restrict ourselves to the living creature, which, in the first place, consists of soul and body: and of these two, the one is by nature the ruler, and the other the subject. But then we must look for the intentions of nature in things which retain their nature, and not in things which are corrupted. And therefore we must study the man who is in the most perfect state both of body and soul, for in him we shall see the true relation of the two; although in bad or corrupted natures the body will often appear to rule over the soul, because they are in an evil and unnatural condition. At all events we may firstly observe in living creatures both a despotical and a constitutional rule; for the soul rules the body with a despotical rule, whereas the intellect rules the appetites with a constitutional and royal rule. And it is clear that the rule of the soul over the body, and of the mind and the rational element over the passionate, is natural and expedient; whereas the equality of the two or the rule of the inferior is always hurtful. The same holds good of animals in relation to men; for tame animals have a better nature than wild, and all tame animals are better off when they are ruled by man; for then they are preserved. Again, the male is by nature superior, and the female inferior; and the one rules, and the other is ruled; this principle, of necessity, extends to all mankind. Where then there is such a difference as that between soul and body, or between men and animals (as in the case of those whose business is to use their body, and who can do nothing better), the lower sort are by nature slaves, and it is better for them as for all inferiors that they should be under the rule of a master. For he who can be, and therefore is, another's, and he who participates in rational principle enough to apprehend, but not to have, such a principle, is a slave by nature. Whereas the lower animals cannot even apprehend a principle; they obey their instincts. And indeed the use made of slaves and of tame animals is not very different; for both with their bodies minister to the needs of life. Nature would like to distinguish between the bodies of freemen and slaves, making the one strong for servile labour, the other upright, and although useless for such services, useful for political life in the arts both of war and peace. But the opposite often happens—that some have the souls and others have the bodies of freemen. And doubtless if men differed from one another in the mere forms of their bodies as much as the statues of the Gods do from men, all would acknowledge that the inferior class should be slaves of the superior. And if this is true of the body, how much more just that a similar distinction should exist in the soul? but the beauty of the body is seen, whereas the beauty of the soul is not seen. It is clear, then, that some men are by nature free, and others slaves, and that for these latter slavery is both expedient and right.

Chapter 6

But that those who take the opposite view have in a certain way right on their side, may be easily seen. For the words slavery and slave are used in two senses. There is a slave or slavery by law as well as by nature. The law of which I speak is a sort of convention—the law by which whatever is taken in war is supposed to belong to the victors. But this right many jurists impeach, as they would an orator who brought forward an unconstitutional measure: they detest the notion that, because one man has the power of doing violence and is superior in brute strength, another shall be his slave and subject. Even among philosophers there is a difference of opinion. The origin of the dispute, and what makes the views invade each other's territory, is as follows: in some sense virtue, when furnished with means, has actually the greatest power of exercising force; and as superior power is only found where there is superior excellence of some kind, power seems to imply virtue, and the dispute to be simply one about justice (for it is due to one party identifying justice with goodwill, while the other identifies it with the mere rule of the stronger). If these views are thus set out separately, the other views have no force or plausibility against the view that the superior in virtue ought to rule, or be master. Others, clinging, as they think, simply to a principle of justice (for law and custom are a sort of justice), assume that slavery in accordance with the custom of war is justified by law, but at the same moment they deny this. For what if the cause of the war be unjust? And again, no one would ever say he is a slave who is unworthy to be a slave. Were this the case, men of the highest rank would be slaves and the children of slaves if they or their parents chance to have been taken captive and sold. Wherefore Hellenes do not like to call Hellenes slaves, but confine the term to barbarians. Yet, in using this language, they really mean the natural slave of whom we spoke at first; for it must be admitted that some are slaves everywhere, others nowhere. The same principle applies to nobility. Hellenes regard themselves as noble everywhere, and not only in their own country, but they deem the barbarians noble only when at home, thereby implying that there are two sorts of nobility and freedom, the one absolute, the other relative. The Helen of Theodectes says:

> "Who would presume to call me servant who am
> on both sides sprung from the stem of the Gods?"

What does this mean but that they distinguish freedom and slavery, noble and humble birth, by the two principles of good and evil? They think that as men and animals beget men and animals, so from good men a good man springs. But this is what nature, though she may intend it, cannot always accomplish.

We see then that there is some foundation for this difference of opinion, and that all are not either slaves by nature or freemen by nature, and also that there is in some cases a marked distinction between the two classes, rendering it expedient and right for the one to be slaves and the others to be masters: the one practising obedience, the others exercising the authority and lordship which nature intended them to have. The abuse of this authority is injurious to both; for the interests of part and whole, of body and soul, are the same, and the slave is a part of the master, a living but separated part of his bodily frame. Hence, where the relation of master and slave between them is natural they are friends and have a common interest, but where it rests merely on law and force the reverse is true.

Chapter 7

The previous remarks are quite enough to show that the rule of a master is not a constitutional rule, and that all the different kinds of rule are not, as some affirm, the same with each other. For there is one rule exercised over subjects who are by nature free, another over subjects who are by nature slaves. The rule of a household is a monarchy, for every house is under one head: whereas constitutional rule is a government of freemen and equals. The master is not called a master because he has science, but because he is of a certain character, and the same remark applies to the slave and the freeman. Still there may be a science for the master and a science for the slave. The science of the slave would be such as the man of Syracuse taught, who made money by instructing slaves in their ordinary duties. And such a knowledge may be carried further, so as to include cookery and similar menial arts. For some duties are of the more necessary, others of the more honorable sort; as the proverb says, "slave before slave, master before master." But all such branches of knowledge are servile. There is likewise a science of the master, which teaches the use of slaves; for the master as such is concerned, not with the acquisition, but with the use of them. Yet this so-called science is not anything great or wonderful; for the master need only know how to order that which the slave must know how to execute. Hence those who are in a position which places them above toil have stewards who attend to their households while they occupy themselves with philosophy or with politics. But the art of acquiring slaves, I mean of justly acquiring them, differs both from the art of the master and the art of the slave, being a species of hunting or war. Enough of the distinction between master and slave.

Chapter 8

Let us now inquire into property generally, and into the art of getting wealth, in accordance with our usual method, for a slave has been shown to be a part of property. The first question is whether the art of getting wealth is the same with the art of managing a household or a part of it, or instrumental to it; and if the last, whether in the way that the art of making shuttles is instrumental to the art of weaving, or in the way that the casting of bronze is instrumental to the art of the statuary, for they are not instrumental in the same way, but the one provides tools and the other material; and by material I mean the substratum out of which any work is made; thus wool is the material of the weaver, bronze of the statuary. Now it is easy to see that the art of household management is not identical with the art of getting wealth, for the one uses the material which the other provides. For the art which uses household stores can be no other than the art of household management. There is, however, a doubt whether the art of getting wealth is a part of household management or a distinct art. If the getter of wealth has to consider whence wealth and property can be procured, but there are many sorts of property and riches, then are husbandry, and the care and provision of food in general, parts of the wealth-getting art or distinct arts? Again, there are many sorts of food, and therefore there are many kinds of lives both of animals and men; they must all have food, and the differences in their food have made differences in their ways of life. For of beasts, some are gregarious, others are solitary; they live in the way which is best adapted to sustain them, accordingly as they are carnivorous or herbivorous or omnivorous: and their habits are determined for them by nature in such a manner that they may obtain with greater facility the food of their choice. But, as different species have different tastes, the same things are not naturally pleasant to all of them; and therefore the lives of carnivorous or herbivorous animals further differ among themselves. In the lives of men too there is a great difference. The laziest are shepherds, who lead an idle life, and get their subsistence without trouble from tame animals; their flocks having to wander from place to place in search of pasture, they are compelled to follow them, cultivating a sort of living farm. Others support themselves by hunting, which is of different kinds. Some, for example, are brigands, others, who dwell near lakes or marshes or rivers or a sea in which there are fish, are fishermen, and others live by the pursuit of birds or wild beasts. The greater number obtain a living from the cultivated fruits of the soil. Such are the modes of subsistence which prevail among those whose industry springs up of itself, and whose food is not acquired by exchange and retail trade—there is the shepherd, the husbandman, the brigand, the fisherman, the hunter. Some gain a comfortable maintenance out of two employments, eking out the deficiencies of one of them by another: thus the life of a shepherd may be combined with that of a brigand, the life of a farmer with that of a hunter. Other modes of life are similarly combined in any way which the needs of men may require. Property, in the sense of a bare livelihood, seems to be given by nature herself to all, both when they are first born, and when they are grown up. For some animals bring forth, together with their offspring, so much food as will last until they are able to supply themselves; of this the verminiparous or oviparous animals are an instance; and the viviparous animals have up to a certain time a supply of food for their young in themselves, which is called milk. In like manner we may infer that, after the birth of animals, plants exist for their sake, and that the other animals exist for the sake of man, the tame for use and food, the wild, if not all, at least the greater part of them, for food, and for the provision of clothing and various instruments. Now if nature makes nothing incomplete, and nothing in vain, the inference must be that she has made all animals for the sake of man. And so, in one point of view, the art of war is a natural art of acquisition, for the art of acquisition includes hunting, an art which we ought to practise against wild beasts, and against men who, though intended by nature to be governed, will not submit; for war of such a kind is naturally just.

Of the art of acquisition then there is one kind which by nature is a part of the management of a household, in so far as the art of household management must either find ready to hand, or itself provide, such things necessary to life, and useful for the community of the family or state, as can be stored. They are the elements of true riches; for the amount of property which is needed for a good life is not unlimited, although Solon in one of his poems says that

"No bound to riches has been fixed for man."

But there is a boundary fixed, just as there is in the other arts; for the instruments of any art are never unlimited, either in number or size, and riches may be defined as a number of instruments to be used in a household or in a state. And so we see that there is a natural art of acquisition which is practised by managers of households and by statesmen, and what is the reason of this.

Chapter 9

There is another variety of the art of acquisition which is commonly and rightly called an art of wealth-getting, and has in fact suggested the notion that riches and property have no limit. Being nearly connected with the preceding, it is often identified with it. But though they are not very different, neither are they the same. The kind already described is given by nature, the other is gained by experience and art.

Let us begin our discussion of the question with the following considerations:

Of everything which we possess there are two uses: both belong to the thing as such, but not in the same manner, for one is the proper, and the other the improper or secondary use of it. For example, a shoe is used for wear, and is used for exchange; both are uses of the shoe. He who gives a shoe in exchange for money or food to him who wants one, does indeed use the shoe as a shoe, but this is not its proper or primary purpose, for a shoe is not made to be an object of barter. The same

may be said of all possessions, for the art of exchange
extends to all of them, and it arises at first from what is
natural, from the circumstance that some have too little, others too much. Hence we may infer that retail
trade is not a natural part of the art of getting wealth;
had it been so, men would have ceased to exchange when
they had enough. In the first community, indeed, which
is the family, this art is obviously of no use, but it begins
to be useful when the society increases. For the members of the family originally had all things in common;
later, when the family divided into parts, the parts
shared in many things, and different parts in different
things, which they had to give in exchange for what they
wanted, a kind of barter which is still practised among
barbarous nations who exchange with one another the
necessaries of life and nothing more; giving and receiving wine, for example, in exchange for corn, and the
like. This sort of barter is not part of the wealth-getting
art and is not contrary to nature, but is needed for the
satisfaction of men's natural wants. The other or more
complex form of exchange grew, as might have been
inferred, out of the simpler. When the inhabitants of
one country became more dependent on those of
another, and they imported what they needed, and
exported what they had too much of, money necessarily
came into use. For the various necessaries of life are not
easily carried about, and hence men agreed to employ in

their dealings with each other something which was intrinsically useful and easily applicable to the purposes of life, for example, iron, silver, and the like. Of this the value was at first measured simply by size and weight, but in process of time they put a stamp upon it, to save the trouble of weighing and to mark the value.

When the use of coin had once been discovered, out of the barter of necessary articles arose the other art of wealth-getting, namely, retail trade; which was at first probably a simple matter, but became more complicated as soon as men learned by experience whence and by what exchanges the greatest profit might be made. Originating in the use of coin, the art of getting wealth is generally thought to be chiefly concerned with it, and to be the art which produces riches and wealth; having to consider how they may be accumulated. Indeed, riches is assumed by many to be only a quantity of coin, because the arts of getting wealth and retail trade are concerned with coin. Others maintain that coined money is a mere sham, a thing not natural, but conventional only, because, if the users substitute another commodity for it, it is worthless, and because it is not useful as a means to any of the necessities of life, and, indeed, he who is rich in coin may often be in want of necessary food. But how can that be wealth of which a man may have a great abundance and yet perish with hunger, like Midas in the fable, whose insatiable prayer turned everything that was set before him into gold?

Hence men seek after a better notion of riches and of the art of getting wealth than the mere acquisition of coin, and they are right. For natural riches and the natural art of wealth-getting are a different thing; in their true form they are part of the management of a household; whereas retail trade is the art of producing wealth, not in every way, but by exchange. And it is thought to be concerned with coin; for coin is the unit of exchange and the measure or limit of it. And there is no bound to the riches which spring from this art of wealth-getting. As in the art of medicine there is no limit to the pursuit of health, and as in the other arts there is no limit to the pursuit of their several ends, for they aim at accomplishing their ends to the uttermost (but of the means there is a limit, for the end is always the limit), so, too, in this art of wealth-getting there is no limit of the end, which is riches of the spurious kind, and the acquisition of wealth. But the art of wealth-getting which consists in household management, on the other hand, has a limit; the unlimited acquisition of wealth is not its business. And, therefore, in one point of view, all riches must have a limit; nevertheless, as a matter of fact, we find the opposite to be the case; for all getters of wealth increase their hoard of coin without limit. The source of the confusion is the near connexion between the two kinds of wealth-getting; in either, the instrument is the same, although the use is different, and so they pass into one another; for each is a use of the same property, but with a difference: accumulation is the end in the one case, but there is a further end in the other. Hence some persons are led to believe that getting wealth is the object of household management, and the whole idea of their lives is that they ought either to increase their money without limit, or at any rate not to lose it. The origin of this disposition in men is that they are intent upon living only, and not upon living well; and, as their desires are unlimited, they also desire that the means of gratifying them should be without limit. Those who do aim at a good life seek the means of obtaining bodily pleasures; and, since the enjoyment of these appears to depend on property, they are absorbed in getting wealth: and so there arises the second species of wealth-getting. For, as their enjoyment is in excess, they seek an art which produces the excess of enjoyment; and, if they are not able to supply their pleasures by the art of getting wealth, they try other arts, using in turn every faculty in a manner contrary to nature. The quality of courage, for example, is not intended to make wealth, but to inspire confidence; neither is this the aim of the general's or of the physician's art; but the one aims at victory and the other at health. Nevertheless, some men turn every quality or art into a means of getting wealth; this they conceive to be the end, and to the promotion of the end they think all things must contribute.

Thus, then, we have considered the art of wealth-getting which is unnecessary, and why men want it; and also the necessary art of wealth-getting, which we have seen to be different from the other, and to be a natural part of the art of managing a household, concerned with the provision of food, not, however, like the former kind, unlimited, but having a limit.

Chapter 10

And we have found the answer to our original question, Whether the art of getting wealth is the business of the manager of a household and of the statesman or not their business?—viz. that wealth is presupposed by them. For as political science does not make men, but takes them from nature and uses them, so too nature provides them with earth or sea or the like as a source of food. At this stage begins the duty of the manager of a household, who has to order the things which nature supplies;—he may be compared to the weaver who has not to make but to use wool, and to know, too, what sort of wool is good and serviceable or bad and unserviceable. Were this otherwise, it would be difficult to see why the art of getting wealth is a part of the management of a household and the art of medicine not; for surely the members of a household must have health just as they must have life or any other necessary. The answer is that as from one point of view the master of the house and the ruler of the state have to consider about health, from another point of view not they but the physician; so in one way the art of household management, in another way the subordinate art, has to consider about wealth. But, strictly speaking, as I have already said, the means of life must be provided beforehand by nature; for the business of nature is to furnish food to that which is born, and the food of the offspring is always what remains over of that from which it is produced. Wherefore the art of getting wealth out of fruits and animals is always natural.

There are two sorts of wealth-getting, as I have said; one is a part of household management, the other is retail trade: the former necessary and honorable, while that which consists in exchange is justly censured; for it is unnatural, and a mode by which men gain from one another. The most hated sort, and with the greatest reason, is usury, which makes a gain out of money itself, and not from the natural object of it. For money was intended to be used in exchange, but not to increase at interest. And this term interest, which means the birth of money from money, is applied to the breeding of money because the offspring resembles the parent. Wherefore of all modes of getting wealth this is the most unnatural.

Chapter 12

Of household management we have seen that there are three parts—one is the rule of a master over slaves, which has been discussed already, another of a father, and the third of a husband. A husband and father, we saw, rules over wife and children, both free, but the rule differs, the rule over his children being a royal, over his wife a constitutional rule. For although there may be exceptions to the order of nature, the male is by nature fitter for command than the female, just as the elder and full-grown is superior to the younger and more immature. But in most constitutional states the citizens rule and are ruled by turns, for the idea of a constitutional state implies that the natures of the citizens are equal, and do not differ at all. Nevertheless, when one rules and the other is ruled we endeavour to create a difference of outward forms and names and titles of respect, which may be illustrated by the saying of Amasis about his foot-pan. The relation of the male to the female is of this kind, but there the inequality is permanent. The rule of a father over his children is royal, for he rules by virtue both of love and of the respect due to age, exercising a kind of royal power. And therefore Homer has appropriately called Zeus "father of Gods and men," because he is the king of them all. For a king is the natural superior of his subjects, but he should be of the same kin or kind with them, and such is the relation of elder and younger, of father and son.

BOOK II

Chapter I

Our purpose is to consider what form of political community is best of all for those who are most able to realize their ideal of life. We must therefore examine not only this but other constitutions, both such as actually exist in well-governed states, and any theoretical forms which are held in esteem; that what is good and useful may be brought to light. And let no one suppose that in seeking for something beyond them we are anxious to make a sophistical display at any cost; we only undertake this inquiry because all the constitutions with which we are acquainted are faulty.

We will begin with the natural beginning of the subject. Three alternatives are conceivable: The members of a state must either have (1) all things or (2) nothing in common, or (3) some things in common and some not. That they should have nothing in common is clearly impossible, for the constitution is a community, and must at any rate have a common place—one city will be in one place, and the citizens are those who share in that one city. But should a well-ordered state have all things, as far as may be, in common, or some only and not others? For the citizens might conceivably have wives and children and property in common, as Socrates proposes in the *Republic* of Plato. Which is better, our present condition, or the proposed new order of society?

Chapter 2

There are many difficulties in the community of women. And the principle on which Socrates rests the necessity of such an institution evidently is not established by his arguments. Further, as a means to the end which he ascribes to the state, the scheme, taken literally is impracticable, and how we are to interpret it is nowhere precisely stated. I am speaking of the premiss from which the argument of Socrates proceeds, "that the greater the unity of the state the better." Is it not obvious that a state may at length attain such a degree of unity as to be no longer a state?—since the nature of a state is to be a plurality, and in tending to greater unity, from being a state, it becomes a family, and from being a family, an individual; for the family may be said to be more than the state, and the individual than the family. So that we ought not to attain this greatest unity even if we could, for it would be the destruction of the state. Again, a state is not made up only of so many men, but of different kinds of men; for similars do not constitute a state. It is not like a military alliance. The usefulness of the latter depends upon its quantity even where there is no difference in quality (for mutual protection is the end aimed at), just as a greater weight of anything is more useful than a less (in like manner, a state differs from a nation, when the nation has not its population organized in villages, but lives an Arcadian sort of life); but the elements out of which a unity is to be formed differ in kind. Wherefore the principle of compensation, as I have already remarked in the *Ethics*, is the salvation of states. Even among freemen and equals this is a principle which must be maintained, for they cannot all rule together, but must change at the end of a year or some other period of time or in some order of succession. The result is that upon this plan they all govern; just as if shoemakers and carpenters were to exchange their occupations, and the same persons did not always continue shoemakers and carpenters. And since it is better that this should be so in politics as well, it is clear that while there should be continuance of the same persons in power where this is possible, yet where this is not possible by reason of the natural equality of the citizens, and at the same time it is just that all should share in the government (whether to govern be a good thing or a bad), an approximation to this is that equals should in turn retire from office and should, apart from official position, be treated alike. Thus the one party rule and the others are ruled in turn, as if they were no longer the same persons. In like manner when they hold office

there is a variety in the offices held. Hence it is evident
that a city is not by nature one in that sense which some
persons affirm; and that what is said to be the greatest
good of cities is in reality their destruction; but surely
the good of things must be that which preserves them.
Again, in another point of view, this extreme unification
of the state is clearly not good; for a family is more self-
sufficing than an individual, and a city than a family,
and a city only comes into being when the community is
large enough to be self-sufficing. If then self-sufficiency
is to be desired, the lesser degree of unity is more desirable than the greater.

Chapter 3

But, even supposing that it were best for the community
to have the greatest degree of unity, this unity is by no
means proved to follow from the fact "of all men saying
'mine' and 'not mine' at the same instant of time,"
which, according to Socrates, is the sign of perfect unity
in a state. For the word "all" is ambiguous. If the meaning be that every individual says "mine" and "not mine"
at the same time, then perhaps the result at which
Socrates aims may be in some degree accomplished;
each man will call the same person his own son and the
same person his own wife, and so of his property and of
all that falls to his lot. This, however, is not the way in
which people would speak who had their wives and

children in common; they would say "all" but not "each." In like manner their property would be described as belonging to them, not severally but collectively. There is an obvious fallacy in the term "all": like some other words, "both," "odd," "even," it is ambiguous, and even in abstract argument becomes a source of logical puzzles. That all persons call the same thing mine in the sense in which each does so may be a fine thing, but it is impracticable; or if the words are taken in the other sense, such a unity in no way conduces to harmony. And there is another objection to the proposal. For that which is common to the greatest number has the least care bestowed upon it. Every one thinks chiefly of his own, hardly at all of the common interest; and only when he is himself concerned as an individual. For besides other considerations, everybody is more inclined to neglect the duty which he expects another to fulfil; as in families many attendants are often less useful than a few. Each citizen will have a thousand sons who will not be his sons individually, but anybody will be equally the son of anybody, and will therefore be neglected by all alike. Further, upon this principle, every one will use the word "mine" of one who is prospering or the reverse, however small a fraction he may himself be of the whole number; the same boy will be "my son," "so and so's son," the son of each of the thousand, or whatever be the number of the citizens; and even about this he will not be positive; for it is impossible to know who chanced to have a child, or whether, if one came into existence, it has survived. But which is better—for each to say "mine" in this way, making a man the same relation to two thousand or ten thousand citizens, or to use the word "mine" in the ordinary and more restricted sense? For usually the same person is called by one man his own son whom another calls his own brother or cousin or kinsman— blood relation or connexion by marriage either of himself or of some relation of his, and yet another his clansman or tribesman; and how much better is it to be the real cousin of somebody than to be a son after Plato's fashion! Nor is there any way of preventing brothers and children and fathers and mothers from sometimes recognizing one another; for children are born like their parents, and they will necessarily be finding indications of their relationship to one another. Geographers declare such to be the fact; they say that in part of Upper Libya, where the women are common, nevertheless the children who are born are assigned to their respective fathers on the ground of their likeness. . . .

BOOK III

Chapter I

He who would inquire into the essence and attributes of various kinds of governments must first of all determine "What is a state?" At present this is a disputed question. Some say that the state has done a certain act; others, no, not the state, but the oligarchy or the tyrant. And the legislator or statesman is concerned entirely with the state; a constitution or government being an arrangement of the inhabitants of a state. But a state is composite, like any other whole made up of many parts;—these are the citizens, who compose it. It is evident, therefore, that we must begin by asking, Who is the citizen, and what is the meaning of the term? For here again there may be a difference of opinion. He who is a citizen in a democracy will often not be a citizen in an oligarchy. Leaving out of consideration those who have been made citizens, or who have obtained the name of citizen in any other accidental manner, we may say, first, that a citizen is not a citizen because he lives in a certain place, for resident aliens and slaves share in the place; nor is he a citizen who has no legal right except that of suing and being sued; for this right may be enjoyed under the provisions of a treaty. Nay, resident aliens in many places do not possess even such rights completely, for they are obliged to have a patron, so that they do but imperfectly participate in citizenship, and we call them citizens only in a qualified sense, as we might apply the term to children who are too young to be on the register, or to old men who have been relieved from state duties. Of these we do not say quite simply that they are citizens, but add in the one case that they are not of age, and in the other, that they are past the age, or something of that sort; the precise expression is immaterial, for our meaning is clear. Similar difficulties to those which I have mentioned may be raised and answered about deprived citizens and about exiles. But the citizen whom we are seeking to define is a citizen in the strictest sense, against whom no such exception can be taken, and his special characteristic is that he shares in the administration of justice, and in offices. Now of offices some are discontinuous, and the same persons are not allowed to hold them twice, or can only hold them after a fixed interval; others have no limit of time—for example, the office of a dicast or ecclesiast. It may, indeed, be argued that these are not magistrates at all, and that their functions give them no share in the government. But surely it is ridiculous to say that those who have the supreme power do not govern. Let us not dwell further upon this, which is a purely verbal question; what we want is a common term including both dicast and ecclesiast. Let us, for the sake of distinction, call it "indefinite office," and we will assume that those who share in such office are citizens. This is the most comprehensive definition of a citizen, and best suits all those who are generally so called.

But we must not forget that things of which the underlying principles differ in kind, one of them being first, another second, another third, have, when regarded in this relation, nothing, or hardly anything, worth mentioning in common. Now we see that governments differ in kind, and that some of them are prior and that others are posterior; those which are faulty or perverted are necessarily posterior to those which are perfect. (What we mean by perversion will be hereafter explained.) The citizen then of necessity differs under each form of government; and our definition is best adapted to the citizen of a democracy; but not necessarily to other states. For in some states the people are not acknowledged, nor have they any regular assembly, but only extraordinary ones; and suits are distributed by sections among the magistrates. At Lacedaemon, for instance, the Ephors determine suits about contracts, which they distribute among themselves, while the elders are judges of homicide, and other causes are decided by other magistrates. A similar principle prevails at Carthage; there certain magistrates decide all causes. We may, indeed, modify our definition of the citizen so as to include these states. In them it is the holder of a definite, not of an indefinite office, who legislates and judges, and to some or all such holders of definite offices is reserved the right of deliberating or judging about some things or about all things. The conception of the citizen now begins to clear up.

He who has the power to take part in the deliberative or judicial administration of any state is said by us to be a citizen of that state; and, speaking generally, a state is a body of citizens sufficing for the purposes of life.

Chapter 2

But in practice a citizen is defined to be one of whom both the parents are citizens; others insist on going further back; say to two or three or more ancestors. This is a short and practical definition; but there are some who raise the further question: How this third or fourth ancestor came to be a citizen? Gorgias of Leontini, partly because he was in a difficulty, partly in irony, said—"Mortars are what is made by the mortar-makers, and the citizens of Larissa are those who are made by the magistrates; for it is their trade to make Larissaeans." Yet the question is really simple, for, if according to the definition just given they shared in the government, they were citizens. This is a better definition than the other. For the words, "born of a father or mother who is a citizen," cannot possibly apply to the first inhabitants or founders of a state.

There is a greater difficulty in the case of those who have been made citizens after a revolution, as by Cleisthenes at Athens after the expulsion of the tyrants, for he enrolled in tribes many metics, both strangers and slaves. The doubt in these cases is, not who is, but whether he who is ought to be a citizen; and there will still be a further doubt, whether he who ought not to be a citizen, is one in fact, for what ought not to be is what is false. Now, there are some who hold office, and yet ought not to hold office, whom we describe as ruling, but ruling unjustly. And the citizen was defined by the fact of his holding some kind of rule or office—he who holds a judicial or legislative office fulfils our definition of a citizen. It is evident, therefore, that the citizens about whom the doubt has arisen must be called citizens.

Chapter 3

Whether they ought to be so or not is a question which is bound up with the previous inquiry. For a parallel question is raised respecting the state, whether a certain act is or is not an act of the state; for example, in the transition from an oligarchy or a tyranny to a democracy. In such cases persons refuse to fulfil their contracts or any other obligations, on the ground that the tyrant, and not the state, contracted them; they argue that some constitutions are established by force, and not for the sake of the common good. But this would apply equally to democracies, for they too may be founded on violence, and then the acts of the democracy will be neither more nor less acts of the state in question than those of an oligarchy or of a tyranny. This question runs up into another:—on what principle shall we ever say that the state is the same, or different? It would be a very superficial view which considered only the place and the inhabitants (for the soil and the population may be separated, and some of the inhabitants may live in one place and some in another). This, however, is not a very serious difficulty; we need only remark that the word "state" is ambiguous.

It is further asked: When are men, living in the same place, to be regarded as a single city—what is the limit? Certainly not the wall of the city, for you might surround all Peloponnesus with a wall. Like this, we may say, is Babylon, and every city that has the compass of a nation rather than a city; Babylon, they say, had been taken for three days before some part of the inhabitants became aware of the fact. This difficulty may, however, with advantage be deferred to another occasion; the statesman has to consider the size of the state, and whether it should consist of more than one nation or not.

Again, shall we say that while the race of inhabitants, as well as their place of abode, remain the same, the city is also the same, although the citizens are always dying and being born, as we call rivers and fountains the same, although the water is always flowing away and coming again? Or shall we say that the generations of men, like the rivers, are the same, but that the state changes? For, since the state is a partnership, and is a partnership of citizens in a constitution, when the form of government changes, and becomes different, then it may be supposed that the state is no longer the same, just as a tragic differs from a comic chorus, although the members of both may be identical. And in this manner we speak of every union or composition of elements as different when the form of their composition alters; for example, a scale containing the same sounds is said to be different, accordingly as the Dorian or the Phrygian mode is employed. And if this is true it is evident that the sameness of the state consists chiefly in the sameness of the constitution, and it may be called or not called by the same name, whether the inhabitants are the same or entirely different. It is quite another question, whether a state ought or ought not to fulfil engagements when the form of government changes.

Chapter 4

There is a point nearly allied to the preceding: Whether the virtue of a good man and a good citizen is the same or not. But, before entering on this discussion, we must certainly first obtain some general notion of the virtue of the citizen. Like the sailor, the citizen is a member of a community. Now, sailors have different functions, for one of them is a rower, another a pilot, and a third a look-out man, a fourth is described by some similar term; and while the precise definition of each individual's virtue applies exclusively to him, there is, at the same time, a common definition applicable to them all. For they have all of them a common object, which is safety in navigation. Similarly, one citizen differs from another, but the salvation of the community is the common business of them all. This community is the constitution; the virtue of the citizen must therefore be relative to the constitution of which he is a member. If, then, there are many forms of government, it is evident that there is not one single virtue of the good citizen which is perfect virtue. But we say that the good man is he who has one single virtue which is perfect virtue. Hence it is evident that the good citizen need not of necessity possess the virtue which makes a good man.

The same question may also be approached by another road, from a consideration of the best constitution. If the state cannot be entirely composed of good men, and yet each citizen is expected to do his own business well, and must therefore have virtue, still, inasmuch as all the citizens cannot be alike, the virtue of the citizen and of the good man cannot coincide. All must have the virtue of the good citizen—thus, and thus only, can the state be perfect; but they will not have the virtue of a good man, unless we assume that in the good state all the citizens must be good.

Again, the state, as composed of unlikes, may be compared to the living being: as the first elements into which a living being is resolved are soul and body, as soul is made up of rational principle and appetite, the family of husband and wife, property of master and slave, so of all these, as well as other dissimilar elements, the state is composed; and, therefore, the virtue of all the citizens cannot possibly be the same, any more than the excellence of the leader of a chorus is the same as that of the performer who stands by his side. I have said enough to show why the two kinds of virtue cannot be absolutely and always the same.

But will there then be no case in which the virtue of the good citizen and the virtue of the good man coincide? To this we answer that the good *ruler* is a good and wise man, and that he who would be a statesman must be a wise man. And some persons say that even the education of the ruler should be of a special kind; for are not the children of kings instructed in riding and military exercises? As Euripides says:

"No subtle arts for me, but what the state requires."

As though there were a special education needed by a ruler. If then the virtue of a good ruler is the same as that of a good man, and we assume further that the subject is a citizen as well as the ruler, the virtue of the good citizen and the virtue of the good man cannot be absolutely the same, although in some cases they may; for the virtue of a ruler differs from that of a citizen. It was the sense of this difference which made Jason say that "he felt hungry when he was not a tyrant," meaning that he could not endure to live in a private station. But, on the other hand, it may be argued that men are praised for knowing both how to rule and how to obey, and he is said to be a citizen of approved virtue who is able to do both. Now if we suppose the virtue of a good man to be that which rules, and the virtue of the citizen to include ruling and obeying, it cannot be said that they are equally worthy of praise. Since, then, it is sometimes thought that the ruler and the ruled must learn different things and not the same, but that the citizen must know and share in them both, the inference is obvious. There is, indeed, the rule of a master, which is concerned with menial offices—the master need not know how to perform these, but may employ others in the execution of them: the other would be degrading; and by the other I mean the power actually to do menial duties, which vary much in character and are executed by various classes of slaves, such, for example, as handicraftsmen, who, as their name signifies, live by the labour of their hands:—under these the mechanic is included. Hence in ancient times, and among some nations, the working classes had no share in the government—a privilege which they only acquired under the extreme democracy. Certainly the good man and the statesman and the good citizen ought not to

learn the crafts of inferiors except for their own occasional use; if they habitually practise them, there will
cease to be a distinction between master and slave.

This is not the rule of which we are speaking; but
there is a rule of another kind, which is exercised over
freemen and equals by birth—a constitutional rule,
which the ruler must learn by obeying, as he would
learn the duties of a general of cavalry by being under
the orders of a general of cavalry, or the duties of a general of infantry by being under the orders of a general
of infantry, and by having had the command of a regi-
ment and of a company. It has been well said that "he
who has never learned to obey cannot be a good com-
mander." The two are not the same, but the good citizen ought to be capable of both; he should know how to
govern like a freeman, and how to obey like a freeman—
these are the virtues of a citizen. And, although the
temperance and justice of a ruler are distinct from those
of a subject, the virtue of a good man will include both;
for the virtue of the good man who is free and also a
subject, e.g. his justice, will not be one but will comprise
distinct kinds, the one qualifying him to rule, the other
to obey, and differing as the temperance and courage of
men and women differ. For a man would be thought a
coward if he had no more courage than a courageous
woman, and a woman would be thought loquacious if
she imposed no more restraint on her conversation than

the good man; and indeed their part in the management of the household is different, for the duty of the one is to acquire, and of the other to preserve. Practical wisdom only is characteristic of the ruler: it would seem that all other virtues must equally belong to ruler and subject. The virtue of the subject is certainly not wisdom, but only true opinion; he may be compared to the maker of the flute, while his master is like the flute-player or user of the flute.

From these considerations may be gathered the answer to the question, whether the virtue of the good man is the same as that of the good citizen, or different, and how far the same, and how far different.

Chapter 5

There still remains one more question about the citizen: Is he only a true citizen who has a share of office, or is the mechanic to be included? If they who hold no office are to be deemed citizens, not every citizen can have this virtue of ruling and obeying; for this man is a citizen. And if none of the lower class are citizens, in which part of the state are they to be placed? For they are not resident aliens, and they are not foreigners. May we not reply, that as far as this objection goes there is no more absurdity in excluding them than in excluding slaves and freedmen from any of the above-mentioned classes? It must be admitted that we cannot consider all those to be citizens who are necessary to the existence of the state; for example, children are not citizen equally with grown-up men, who are citizens absolutely, but children, not being grown up, are only citizens on a certain assumption. Nay, in ancient times, and among some nations, the artisan class *were* slaves or foreigners, and therefore the majority of them are so now. The best form of state will not admit them to citizenship; but if they are admitted, then our definition of the virtue of a citizen will not apply to every citizen, nor to every free man as such, but only to those who are freed from necessary services. The necessary people are either slaves who minister to the wants of individuals, or mechanics and labourers who are the servants of the community. These reflections carried a little further will explain their position; and indeed what has been said already is of itself, when understood, explanation enough.

Since there are many forms of government there must be many varieties of citizen and especially of citizens who are subjects; so that under some governments the mechanic and the labourer will be citizens, but not in others, as, for example, in aristocracy or the so-called government of the best (if there be such an one), in which honors are given according to virtue and merit; for no man can practise virtue who is living the life of a mechanic or labourer. In oligarchies the qualification for office is high, and therefore no labourer can ever be a citizen; but a mechanic may, for an actual majority of them are rich. At Thebes there was a law that no man could hold office who had not retired from business for ten years. But in many states the law goes to the length of admitting aliens; for in some democracies a man is a citizen though his mother only be a citizen; and a similar principle is applied to illegitimate children; the law is relaxed when there is a dearth of population. But when the number of citizens increases, first the children of a male or a female slave are excluded; then those whose mothers only are citizens; and at last the right of citizenship is confined to those whose fathers and mothers are both citizens.

Hence, as is evident, there are different kinds of citizens; and he is a citizen in the highest sense who shares in the honors of the state. Compare Homer's words, "like some dishonored stranger"; he who is excluded from the honors of the state is no better than an alien. But when his exclusion is concealed, then the object is that the privileged class may deceive their fellow inhabitants.

As to the question whether the virtue of the good man is the same as that of the good citizen, the considerations already adduced prove that in some states the good man and the good citizen are the same, and in others different. When they are the same it is not every citizen who is a good man, but only the statesman and those who have or may have, alone or in conjunction with others, the conduct of public affairs.

Chapter 6

Having determined these questions, we have next to consider whether there is only one form of government or many, and if many, what they are, and how many, and what are the differences between them.

A constitution is the arrangement of magistracies in a state, especially of the highest of all. The government is everywhere sovereign in the state, and the constitution is in fact the government. For example, in democracies the people are supreme, but in oligarchies, the few; and, therefore, we say that these two forms of government also are different: and so in other cases.

First, let us consider what is the purpose of a state, and how many forms of government there are by which human society is regulated. We have already said, in the first part of this treatise, when discussing household management and the rule of a master, that man is by nature a political animal. And therefore, men, even when they do not require one another's help, desire to live together; not but that they are also brought together by their common interests in proportion as they severally attain to any measure of well-being. This is certainly the chief end, both of individuals and of states. And also for the sake of mere life (in which there is possibly some noble element so long as the evils of existence do not greatly overbalance the good) mankind meet together and maintain the political community. And we all see that men cling to life even at the cost of enduring great misfortune, seeming to find in life a natural sweetness and happiness.

There is no difficulty in distinguishing the various kinds of authority; they have been often defined already in discussions outside the school. The rule of a master, although the slave by nature and the master by nature have in reality the same interests, is nevertheless exercised primarily with a view to the interest of the master, but accidentally considers the slave, since, if the slave perish, the rule of the master perishes with him. On the other hand, the government of a wife and children and of a household, which we have called household management, is exercised in the first instance for the good of the governed or for the common good of both parties, but essentially for the good of the governed, as we see to be the case in medicine, gymnastic, and the arts in general, which are only accidentally concerned with the good of the artists themselves. For there is no reason why the trainer may not sometimes practise gymnastics, and the helmsman is always one of the crew. The trainer or the helmsman considers the good of those committed to his care. But, when he is one of the persons taken care of, he accidentally participates in the advantage, for the helmsman is also a sailor, and the trainer becomes one of those in training. And so in politics: when the state is framed upon the principle of equality and likeness, the citizens think that they ought to hold office by turns. Formerly, as is natural, every one would take his turn of service; and then again, somebody else would look after his interest, just as he, while in office, had looked after theirs. But nowadays, for the sake of the advantage which is to be gained from the public revenues and from office, men want to be always in office. One might imagine that the rulers, being sickly, were only kept in health while they continued in office; in that case we may be sure that they would be hunting after places. The conclusion is evident: that governments which have a regard to the common interest are constituted in accordance with strict principles of justice, and are therefore true forms; but those which regard only the interest of the rulers are all defective and perverted forms, for they are despotic, whereas a state is a community of freemen.

Chapter 7

Having determined these points, we have next to consider how many forms of government there are, and what they are; and in the first place what are the true forms, for when they are determined the perversions of them will at once be apparent. The words constitution and government have the same meaning, and the government, which is the supreme authority in states, must be in the hands of one, or of a few, or of the many. The true forms of government, therefore, are those in which the one, or the few, or the many, govern with a view to the common interest; but governments which rule with a view to the private interest, whether of the one, or of the few, or of the many, are perversions. For the members of a state, if they are truly citizens, ought to participate in its advantages. Of forms of government in which one rules, we call that which regards the common interests, kingship or royalty; that in which more than one, but not many, rule, aristocracy; and it is so called, either because the rulers are the best men, or because they have at heart the best interests of the state and of the citizens. But when the citizens at large administer the state for the common interest, the government is called by the generic name—a constitution. And there is a reason for this use of language. One man or a few may excel in virtue; but as the number increases it becomes more difficult for them to attain perfection in every kind of virtue, though they may in military virtue, for this is found in the masses. Hence in a constitutional government the fighting-men have the supreme power, and those who possess arms are the citizens.

Of the above-mentioned forms, the perversions are as follows:—of royalty, tyranny; of aristocracy, oligarchy; of constitutional government, democracy. For tyranny is a kind of monarchy which has in view the interest of the monarch only; oligarchy has in view the interest of the wealthy; democracy, of the needy: none of them the common good of all.

Chapter 8

But there are difficulties about these forms of government, and it will therefore be necessary to state a little more at length the nature of each of them. For he who would make a philosophical study of the various sciences, and does not regard practice only, ought not to overlook or omit anything, but to set forth the truth in every particular. Tyranny, as I was saying, is monarchy exercising the rule of a master over the political society; oligarchy is when men of property have the government in their hands; democracy, the opposite, when the indigent, and not the men of property, are the rulers. And here arises the first of our difficulties, and it relates to the distinction just drawn. For democracy is said to be the government of the many. But what if the many are men of property and have the power in their hands? In like manner oligarchy is said to be the government of the few; but what if the poor are fewer than the rich, and have the power in their hands because they are stronger? In these cases the distinction which we have drawn between these different forms of government would no longer hold good.

Suppose, once more, that we add wealth to the few and poverty to the many, and name the governments accordingly—an oligarchy is said to be that in which the few and the wealthy, and a democracy that in which the many and the poor are the rulers—there will still be a difficulty. For, if the only forms of government are the ones already mentioned, how shall we describe those other governments also just mentioned by us, in which the rich are the more numerous and the poor are the fewer, and both govern in their respective states?

The argument seems to show that, whether in oligarchies or in democracies, the number of the governing body, whether the greater number, as in a democracy, or the smaller number, as in an oligarchy, is an accident due to the fact that the rich everywhere are few, and the poor numerous. But if so, there is a misapprehension of the causes of the difference between them. For the real difference between democracy and oligarchy is poverty and wealth. Wherever men rule by reason of their wealth, whether they be few or many, that is an oligarchy, and where the poor rule, that is a democracy. But as a fact the rich are few and the poor many; for few are well-to-do, whereas freedom is enjoyed by all, and wealth and freedom are the grounds on which the oligarchical and democratical parties respectively claim power in the state.

Chapter 9

Let us begin by considering the common definitions of oligarchy and democracy, and what is justice oligarchical and democratical. For all men cling to justice of some kind, but their conceptions are imperfect and they do not express the whole idea. For example, justice is thought by them to be, and is, equality, not, however, for all, but only for equals. And inequality is thought to be, and is, justice; neither is this for all, but only for unequals. When the persons are omitted, then men judge erroneously. The reason is that they are passing judgement on themselves, and most people are bad judges in their own case. And whereas justice implies a relation to persons as well as to things, and a just distribution, as I have already said in the *Ethics*, implies the same ratio between the persons and between the things, they agree about the equality of the things, but dispute about the equality of the persons, chiefly for the reason which I have just given—because they are bad judges in their own affairs; and secondly, because both the parties to the argument are speaking of a limited and partial justice, but imagine themselves to be speaking of absolute justice. For the one party, if they are unequal in one respect, for example wealth, consider themselves to be unequal in all; and the other party, if they are equal in one respect, for example free birth, consider themselves to be equal in all. But they leave out the capital point. For if men met and associated out of regard to wealth only, their share in the state would be proportioned to their property, and the oligarchical doctrine would then seem to carry the day. It would not be just that he who paid one mina should have the same share of a hundred minae, whether of the principal or of the profits, as he who paid the remaining ninety-nine. But a state exists for the sake of a good life, and not for the sake of life only: if life only were the object, slaves and brute animals might form a state, but they cannot, for they have no share in happiness or in a life of free choice. Nor does a state exist for the sake of alliance and security from injustice, nor yet for the sake of exchange and mutual intercourse; for then the Tyrrhenians and the Carthaginians, and all who have commercial treaties with one another, would be the citizens of one state. True, they have agreements about imports, and engagements that they will do no wrong to one another, and written articles of alliance. But there are no magistracies common to the contracting parties who will enforce their engagements; different states have each their own magistracies. Nor does one state take care that the citizens of the other are such as they ought to be, nor see that those who come under the terms of the treaty do no wrong or wickedness at all, but only that they do no injustice to one another. Whereas, those who care for good government take into consideration virtue and vice in states. Whence it may be further inferred that virtue must be the care of a state which is truly so called, and not merely enjoys the name: for without this end the community becomes a mere alliance which differs only in place from alliances of which the members live apart; and law is only a convention, "a surety to one another of justice," as the sophist Lycophron says, and has no real power to make the citizens

This is obvious; for suppose distinct places, such as Corinth and Megara, to be brought together so that their walls touched, still they would not be one city, not even if the citizens had the right to intermarry, which is one of the rights peculiarly characteristic of states. Again, if men dwelt at a distance from one another, but not so far off as to have no intercourse, and there were laws among them that they should not wrong each other in their exchanges, neither would this be a state. Let us suppose that one man is a carpenter, another a husbandman, another a shoemaker, and so on, and that their number is ten thousand: nevertheless, if they have nothing in common but exchange, alliance, and the like, that would not constitute a state. Why is this? Surely not because they are at a distance from one another: for even supposing that such a community were to meet in one place, but that each man had a house of his own, which was in a manner his state, and that they made alliance with one another, but only against evil-doers; still an accurate thinker would not deem this to be a state, if their intercourse with one another was of the same character after as before their union. It is clear then that a state is not a mere society, having a common place, established for the prevention of mutual crime and for the sake of exchange. These are conditions without which a state cannot exist; but all of them together do not constitute a state, which is a community of families and aggregations of families in well-being, for the sake of a perfect and self-sufficing life. Such a community can only be established among those who live in the same place and intermarry. Hence arise in cities family connexions, brotherhoods, common sacrifices, amusements which draw men together. But these are created by friendship, for the will to live together is friendship. The end of the state is the good life, and these are the means towards it. And the state is the union of families and villages in a perfect and self-sufficing life, by which we mean a happy and honorable life.

Our conclusion, then, is that political society exists for the sake of noble actions, and not of mere companionship. Hence they who contribute most to such a society have a greater share in it than those who have the same or a greater freedom or nobility of birth but are inferior to them in political virtue; or than those who exceed them in wealth but are surpassed by them in virtue.

From what has been said it will be clearly seen that all the partisans of different forms of government speak of a part of justice only.

Chapter 13

If the existence of the state is alone to be considered, then it would seem that all, or some at least, of these claims are just; but, if we take into account a good life, then, as I have already said, education and virtue have superior claims. As, however, those who are equal in one thing ought not to have an equal share in all, nor those who are unequal in one thing to have an unequal share in all, it is certain that all forms of government which rest on either of these principles are perversions. All men have a claim in a certain sense, as I have already admitted, but all have not an absolute claim. The rich claim because they have a greater share in the land, and land is the common element of the state; also they are generally more trustworthy in contracts. The free claim under the same tide as the noble; for they are nearly akin. For the noble are citizens in a truer sense than the ignoble, and good birth is always valued in a man's own home and country. Another reason is, that those who are sprung from better ancestors are likely to be better men, for nobility is excellence of race. Virtue, too, may be truly said to have a claim, for justice has been acknowledged by us to be a social virtue, and it implies all others. Again, the many may urge their claim against the few; for, when taken collectively, and compared with the few, they are stronger and richer and better. But, what if the good, the rich, the noble, and the other classes who make up a state, are all living together in the same city, will there, or will there not, be any doubt who shall rule?—No doubt at all in determining who ought to rule in each of the above-mentioned forms of government. For states are characterized by differences in their governing bodies—one of them has a government of the rich, another of the virtuous, and so on. But a difficulty arises when all these elements coexist. How are we to decide? Suppose the virtuous to be very few in number: may we consider their numbers in relation to their duties, and ask whether they are enough to administer the state, or so many as will make up a state? Objections may be urged against all the aspirants to political power. For those who found their claims on wealth or family might be thought to have no basis of justice; on this principle, if any one person were richer than all the rest, it is clear that he ought to be ruler of them. In like manner he who is very distinguished by his birth ought to have the superiority over all those who claim on the ground that they are freeborn. In an aristocracy, or government of the best, a like difficulty occurs about virtue; for if one citizen be better than the other members of the government, however good they may be, he too, upon the same principle of justice, should rule over them. And if the people are to be supreme because they are stronger than the few, then if one man, or more than one, but not a majority, is stronger than the many, they ought to rule, and not the many.

All these considerations appear to show that none of the principles on which men claim to rule and to hold all other men in subjection to them are strictly right. To those who claim to be masters of the government on the ground of their virtue or their wealth, the many might fairly answer that they themselves are often better and richer than the few—I do not say individually, but collectively. And another ingenious objection which is sometimes put forward may be met in a similar manner. Some persons doubt whether the legislator who desires to make the justest laws ought to legislate with a view to the good of the higher classes or of the many, when the case which we have mentioned occurs. Now what is just or right is to be interpreted in the sense of "what is equal"; and that which is right in the sense of being equal is to be considered with reference to the advantage of the state, and the common good of the citizens. And a citizen is one who shares in governing and being governed. He differs under different forms of government, but in the best state he is one who is able and willing to be governed and to govern with a view to the life of virtue.

If, however, there be some one person, or more than one, although not enough to make up the full complement of a state, whose virtue is so pre-eminent that the virtues or the political capacity of all the rest admit of no comparison with his or theirs, he or they can be no longer regarded as part of a state; for justice will not be done to the superior, if he is reckoned only as the equal of those who are so far inferior to him in virtue and in political capacity. Such an one may truly be deemed a God among men. Hence we see that legislation is necessarily concerned only with those who are equal in birth and in capacity; and that for men of pre-eminent virtue there is no law—they are themselves a law. Any one would be ridiculous who attempted to make laws for them: they would probably retort what, in the fable of Antisthenes, the lions said to the hares, when in the council of the beasts the latter began haranguing and claiming equality for all. And for this reason democratic states have instituted ostracism; equality is above all things their aim, and therefore they ostracized and banished from the city for a time those who seemed to predominate too much through their wealth, or the number of their friends, or through any other political influence. Mythology tells us that the Argonauts left

Heracles behind for a similar reason; the ship Argo would not take him because she feared that he would have been too much for the rest of the crew. Wherefore those who denounce tyranny and blame the counsel which Periander gave to Thrasybulus cannot be held altogether just in their censure. The story is that Perian der, when the herald was sent to ask counsel of him, said nothing, but only cut off the tallest ears of corn till he had brought the field to a level. The herald did not know the meaning of the action, but came and reported what he had seen to Thrasybulus, who understood that he was to cut off the principal men in the state; and this is a policy not only expedient for tyrants or in practice confined to them, but equally necessary in oligarchies and democracies. Ostracism is a measure of the same kind, which acts by disabling and banishing the most prominent citizens. Great powers do the same to whole cities and nations, as the Athenians did to the Samians, Chians, and Lesbians; no sooner had they obtained a firm grasp of the empire, than they humbled their allies contrary to treaty; and the Persian king has repeatedly crushed the Medes, Babylonians, and other nations, when their spirit has been stirred by the recollection of their former greatness.

The problem is a universal one, and equally concerns all forms of government, true as well as false; for, although perverted forms with a view to their own interests may adopt this policy, those which seek the common interest do so likewise. The same thing may be observed in the arts and sciences; for the painter will not allow the figure to have a foot which, however beautiful, is not in proportion, nor will the ship-builder allow the stern or any other part of the vessel to be unduly large, any more than the chorus-master will allow any one who sings louder or better than all the rest to sing in the choir. Monarchs, too, may practise compulsion and still live in harmony with their cities, if their own government is for the interest of the state. Hence where there is an acknowledged superiority the argument in favour of ostracism is based upon a kind of political justice. It would certainly be better that the legislator should from the first so order his state as to have no need of such a remedy. But if the need arises, the next best thing is that he should endeavour to correct the evil by this or some similar measure. The principle, however, has not been fairly applied in states; for, instead of looking to the good of their own constitution, they have used ostracism for factious purposes. It is true that under perverted forms of government, and from their special point of view, such a measure is just and expedient, but it is also clear that it is not absolutely just. In the perfect state there would be great doubts about the use of it, not when applied to excess in strength, wealth, popularity, or the like, but when used against some one who is pre-eminent in virtue—what is to be done with him? Mankind will not say that such an one is to be expelled and exiled; on the other hand, he ought not to be a subject—that would be as if mankind should claim to rule over Zeus, dividing his offices among them. The only alternative is that all should joyfully obey such a ruler, according to what seems to be the order of nature, and that men like him should be kings in their state for life.

Chapter 14

The preceding discussion, by a natural transition, leads to the consideration of royalty, which we admit to be one of the true forms of government. Let us see whether in order to be well governed a state or country should be under the rule of a king or under some other form of government; and whether monarchy, although good for some, may not be bad for others. But first we must determine whether there is one species of royalty or many. It is easy to see that there are many, and that the manner of government is not the same in all of them.

Of royalties according to law, (I) the Lacedaemonian is thought to answer best to the true pattern; but there the royal power is not absolute, except when the kings go on an expedition, and then they take the command. Matters of religion are likewise committed to them. The kingly office is in truth a kind of generalship, irresponsible and perpetual. The king has not the power of life and death, except in a specified case, as for instance, in ancient times, he had it when upon a campaign, by right of force. This custom is described in Homer. For Agamemnon is patient when he is attacked in the assembly, but when the army goes out to battle he has the power even of life and death. Does he not say?—"When I find a man skulking apart from the battle, nothing shall save him from the dogs and vultures, for in my hands is death."

This, then, is one form of royalty—a generalship for life: and of such royalties some are hereditary and others elective.

(2) There is another sort of monarchy not uncommon among the barbarians, which nearly resembles tyranny. But this is both legal and hereditary. For barbarians, being more servile in character than Hellenes, and Asiatics than Europeans, do not rebel against a despotic government. Such royalties have the nature of tyrannies because the people are by nature slaves; but there is no danger of their being overthrown, for they are hereditary and legal. Wherefore also their guards are such as a king and not such as a tyrant would employ, that is to say, they are composed of citizens, whereas the guards of tyrants are mercenaries. For kings rule according to law over voluntary subjects, but tyrants over involuntary; and the one are guarded by their fellow-citizens, the others are guarded against them.

These are two forms of monarchy, and there was a third (3) which existed in ancient Hellas, called an Aesymnetia or dictatorship. This may be defined generally as an elective tyranny, which, like the barbarian monarchy, is legal, but differs from it in not being hereditary. Sometimes the office was held for life, sometimes for a term of years, or until certain duties had been performed. For example, the Mytilenaeans elected Pittacus leader against the exiles, who were headed by Antimenides and Alcaeus the poet. And Alcaeus himself shows in one of his banquet odes that they chose Pittacus tyrant, for he reproaches his fellow-citizens for "having made the low-born Pittacus tyrant of the spiritless and ill-fated city, with one voice shouting his praises."

These forms of government have always had the character of tyrannies, because they possess despotic power; but inasmuch as they are elective and acquiesced in by their subjects, they are kingly.

(4) There is a fourth species of kingly rule—that of the heroic times—which was hereditary and legal, and was exercised over willing subjects. For the first chiefs were benefactors of the people in arts or arms; they either gathered them into a community, or procured land for them; and thus they became kings of voluntary subjects, and their power was inherited by their descendants. They took the command in war and presided

over the sacrifices, except those which required a priest. They also decided causes either with or without an oath; and when they swore, the form of the oath was the stretching out of their sceptre. In ancient times their power extended continuously to all things whatsoever, in city and country, as well as in foreign parts; but at a later date they relinquished several of these privileges, and others the people took from them, until in some states nothing was left to them but the sacrifices; and where they retained more of the reality they had only the right of leadership in war beyond the border.

These, then, are the four kinds of royalty. First the monarchy of the heroic ages; this was exercised over voluntary subjects, but limited to certain functions; the king was a general and a judge, and had the control of religion The second is that of the barbarians, which is an hereditary despotic government in accordance with law. A third is the power of the so-called Aesymnete or Dictator; this is an elective tyranny. The fourth is the Lacedaemonian, which is in fact a generalship, hereditary and perpetual. These four forms differ from one another in the manner which I have described.

(5) There is a fifth form of kingly rule in which one has the disposal of all, just as each nation or each state has the disposal of public matters; this form corresponds to the control of a household. For as household management is the kingly rule of a house, so kingly rule

is the household management of a city, or of a nation, or of many nations.

Chapter 18

We maintain that the true forms of government are three, and that the best must be that which is administered by the best, and in which there is one man, or a whole family, or many persons, excelling all the others together in virtue, and both rulers and subjects are fitted, the one to rule, the others to be ruled, in such a manner as to attain the most eligible life. We showed at the commencement of our inquiry that the virtue of the good man is necessarily the same as the virtue of the citizen of the perfect state. Clearly then in the same manner, and by the same means through which a man becomes truly good, he will frame a state that is to be ruled by an aristocracy, statesman or king.

BOOK IV

Chapter II

We have now to inquire what is the best constitution for most states, and the best life for most men, neither assuming a standard of virtue which is above ordinary persons, nor an education which is exceptionally favoured by nature and circumstances, nor yet an ideal state which is an aspiration only, but having regard to the life in which the majority are able to share, and to the form of government which states in general can attain. As to those aristocracies, as they are called, of which we were just now speaking, they either lie beyond the possibilities of the greater number of states, or they approximate to the so-called constitutional government, and therefore need no separate discussion. And in fact the conclusion at which we arrive respecting all these forms rests upon the same grounds. For if what was said in the *Ethics* is true, that the happy life is the life according to virtue lived without impediment, and that virtue is a mean, then the life which is in a mean, and in a mean attainable by every one, must be the best. And the same principles of virtue and vice are characteristic of cities and of constitutions; for the constitution is in a figure the life of the city.

Now in all states there are three elements: one class is very rich, another very poor, and a third in a mean. It is admitted that moderation and the mean are best, and therefore it will clearly be best to possess the gifts of fortune in moderation; for in that condition of life men are most ready to follow rational principle. But he who greatly excels in beauty, strength, birth, or wealth, or on the other hand who is very poor, or very weak, or very much disgraced, finds it difficult to follow rational principle. Of these two the one sort grow into violent and great criminals, the others into rogues and petty rascals. And two sorts of offences correspond to them,

the one committed from violence, the other from rogu-
ery. Again, the middle class is least likely to shrink from
rule, or to be over-ambitious for it; both of which are
injuries to the state. Again, those who have too much of
the goods of fortune, strength, wealth, friends, and the
like, are neither willing nor able to submit to authority.
The evil begins at home; for when they are boys, by
reason of the luxury in which they are brought up, they
never learn, even at school, the habit of obedience. On
the other hand, the very poor, who are in the opposite
extreme, are too degraded. So that the one class cannot
obey, and can only rule despotically; the other knows
not how to command and must be ruled like slaves.
Thus arises a city, not of freemen, but of masters and
slaves, the one despising, the other envying; and nothing can be more fatal to friendship and good fellowship
in states than this: for good fellowship springs from
friendship; when men are at enmity with one another,
they would rather not even share the same path. But a
city ought to be composed, as far as possible, of equals
and similars; and these are generally the middle classes.
Wherefore the city which is composed of middle-class
citizens is necessarily best constituted in respect of the
elements of which we say the fabric of the state naturally consists. And this is the class of citizens which is
most secure in a state, for they do not, like the poor,
covet their neighbours' goods; nor do others covet

theirs, as the poor covet the goods of the rich; and as they neither plot against others, nor are themselves plotted against, they pass through life safely. Wisely then did Phocylides pray—"Many things are best in the mean; I desire to be of a middle condition in my city."

Thus it is manifest that the best political community is formed by citizens of the middle class, and that those states are likely to be well-administered, in which the middle class is large, and stronger if possible than both the other classes, or at any rate than either singly; for the addition of the middle class turns the scale, and prevents either of the extremes from being dominant. Great then is the good fortune of a state in which the citizens have a moderate and sufficient property; for where some possess much, and the others nothing, there may arise an extreme democracy, or a pure oligarchy; or a tyranny may grow out of either extreme—either out of the most rampant democracy, or out of an oligarchy; but it is not so likely to arise out of the middle constitutions and those akin to them. I will explain the reason of this hereafter, when I speak of the revolutions of states. The mean condition of states is clearly best, for no other is free from faction; and where the middle class is large, there are least likely to be factions and dissensions. For a similar reason large states are less liable to faction than small ones, because in them the middle class is large; whereas in small states it is easy to divide all the citizens into two classes who are either rich or poor, and to leave nothing in the middle. And democracies are safer and more permanent than oligarchies, because they have a middle class which is more numerous and has a greater share in the government; for when there is no middle class, and the poor greatly exceed in number, troubles arise, and the state soon comes to an end. A proof of the superiority of the middle class is that the best legislators have been of a middle condition; for example, Solon, as his own verses testify; and Lycurgus, for he was not a king; and Charondas, and almost all legislators.

These considerations will help us to understand why most governments are either democratical or oligarchical. The reason is that the middle class is seldom numerous in them, and whichever party, whether the rich or the common people, transgresses the mean and predominates, draws the constitution its own way, and thus arises either oligarchy or democracy. There is another reason—the poor and the rich quarrel with one another, and whichever side gets the better, instead of establishing a just or popular government, regards political supremacy as the prize of victory, and the one party sets up a democracy and the other an oligarchy. Further, both the parties which had the supremacy in Hellas looked only to the interest of their own form of government, and established in states, the one, democracies, and the other, oligarchies; they thought of their own advantage, of the public not at all. For these reasons the middle form of government has rarely, if ever, existed, and among a very few only. One man alone of all who ever ruled in Hellas was induced to give this middle constitution to states. But it has now become a habit among the citizens of states, not even to care about equality; all men are seeking for dominion, or, if conquered, are willing to submit.

What then is the best form of government, and what makes it the best, is evident; and of other constitutions, since we say that there are many kinds of democracy and many of oligarchy, it is not difficult to see which has the first and which the second or any other place in the order of excellence, now that we have determined which is the best. For that which is nearest to the best must of necessity be better, and that which is furthest from it worse, if we are judging absolutely and not relatively to given conditions: I say "relatively to given conditions," since a particular government may be preferable, but another form may be better for some people.

Chapter 12

We have now to consider what and what kind of government is suitable to what and what kind of men. I may begin by assuming, as a general principle common to all governments, that the portion of the state which desires the permanence of the constitution ought to be stronger than that which desires the reverse. Now every city is composed of quality and quantity. By quality I mean freedom, wealth, education, good birth, and by quantity, superiority of numbers. Quality may exist in one of the classes which make up the state, and quantity in the other. For example, the meanly-born may be more in number than the well-born, or the poor than the rich, yet they may not so much exceed in quantity as they fall short in quality; and therefore there must be a comparison of quantity and quality. Where the number of the poor is more than proportioned to the wealth of the rich, there will naturally be a democracy, varying in form with the sort of people who compose it in each case. If, for example, the husbandmen exceed in number, the first form of democracy will then arise; if the artisans and labouring class, the last; and so with the intermediate forms. But where the rich and the notables exceed in quality more than they fall short in quantity, there oligarchy arises, similarly assuming various forms according to the kind of superiority possessed by the oligarchs.

The legislator should always include the middle class in his government; if he makes his laws oligarchical, to the middle class let him look; if he makes them democratical, he should equally by his laws try to attach this class to the state. There only can the government ever be stable where the middle class exceeds one or both of the others, and in that case there will be no fear that the rich will unite with the poor against the rulers. For neither of them will ever be willing to serve the other, and if they look for some form of government more suitable to both, they will find none better than this, for the rich and the poor will never consent to rule in turn, because they mistrust one another. The arbiter is always the one trusted, and he who is in the middle is an arbiter. The more perfect the admixture of the political elements, the more lasting will be the constitution. Many even of those who desire to form aristocratical governments make a mistake, not only in giving too much power to the rich, but in attempting to overreach the people. There comes a time when out of a false good there arises a true evil, since the encroachments of the rich are more destructive to the constitution than those of the people.

BOOK V

Chapter I

The design which we proposed to ourselves is now nearly completed. Next in order follow the causes of revolution in states, how many, and of what nature they are; what modes of destruction apply to particular states, and out of what, and into what they mostly change; also what are the modes of preservation in states generally, or in a particular state, and by what means each state may be best preserved: these questions remain to be considered.

. . . As I was saying before, men agree that justice in the abstract is proportion, but they differ in that some think that if they are equal in any respect they are equal absolutely, others that if they are unequal in any respect they should be unequal in all. Hence there are two principal forms of government, democracy and oligarchy; for good birth and virtue are rare, but wealth and numbers are more common. In what city shall we find a hundred persons of good birth and virtue? Whereas the rich everywhere abound. That a state should be ordered, simply and wholly, according to either kind of equality, is not a good thing; the proof is the fact that such forms of government never last. They are originally based on a mistake, and, as they begin badly, cannot fail to end badly. . . .

Still democracy appears to be safer and less liable to revolution than oligarchy. For in oligarchies there is the double danger of the oligarchs falling out among themselves and also with the people; but in democracies there is only one danger of a quarrel with the oligarchs. No dissension worth mentioning arises among the people themselves. And we may further remark that a government which is composed of the middle class more nearly approximates to democracy than oligarchy, and is the safest of the imperfect forms of government.

Chapter 3

What share insolence and avarice have in creating revolutions, and how they work, is plain enough. When the magistrates are insolent and grasping they conspire against one another and also against the constitution from which they derive their power, making their gains either at the expense of individuals or of the public. It is evident, again, what an influence honor exerts and how it is a cause of revolution. Men who are themselves dishonored and who see others obtaining honors rise in rebellion; the honor or dishonor when undeserved is unjust; and just when awarded according to merit. Again, superiority is a cause of revolution when one or more persons have a power which is too much for the state and the power of the government; this is a condition of affairs out of which there arises a monarchy, or a family oligarchy. And therefore, in some places, as at Athens and Argos, they have recourse to ostracism. But how much better to provide from the first that there should be no such pre-eminent individuals instead of letting them come into existence and then finding a remedy.

Another cause of revolution is fear. Either men have committed wrong, and are afraid of punishment, or they are expecting to suffer wrong and are desirous of anticipating their enemy. Thus at Rhodes the notables conspired against the people through fear of the suits that were brought against them. Contempt is also a cause of insurrection and revolution; for example, in oligarchies—when those who have no share in the state are the majority, they revolt, because they think that they are the stronger. Or, again, in democracies, the rich despise the disorder and anarchy of the state; at Thebes, for example, where, after the battle of Oenophyta, the bad administration of the democracy led to its ruin. At Megara the fall of the democracy was due to a defeat occasioned by disorder and anarchy. And at Syracuse the democracy aroused contempt before the tyranny of Gelo arose; at Rhodes, before the insurrection.

Chapter 4

In revolutions the occasions may be trifling, but great interests are at stake. Even trifles are most important when they concern the rulers, as was the case of old at Syracuse; for the Syracusan constitution was once changed by a love-quarrel of two young men, who were in the government. The story is that while one of them was away from home his beloved was gained over by his companion, and he to revenge himself seduced the other's wife. They then drew the members of the ruling class into their quarrel and so split all the people into portions. We learn from this story that we should be on our guard against the beginnings of such evils, and should put an end to the quarrels of chiefs and mighty men. The mistake lies in the beginning—as the proverb says— "Well begun is half done"; so an error at the beginning, though quite small, bears the same ratio to the errors in the other parts. In general, when the notables quarrel, the whole city is involved, as happened in Hestiaea after the Persian War. The occasion was the division of an inheritance; one of two brothers refused to give an account of their father's property and the treasure which he had found: so the poorer of the two quarrelled with him and enlisted in his cause the popular party, the other, who was very rich, the wealthy classes. . . .

Chapter 5

And now, taking each constitution separately, we must see what follows from the principles already laid down.

Revolutions in democracies are generally caused by the intemperance of demagogues, who either in their private capacity lay information against rich men until they compel them to combine (for a common danger unites even the bitterest enemies), or coming forward in public stir up the people against them. The truth of this remark is proved by a variety of examples. At Cos the democracy was overthrown because wicked demagogues arose, and the notables combined. At Rhodes the demagogues not only provided pay for the multitude, but prevented them from making good to the trierarchs the sums which had been expended by them; and they, in consequence of the suits which were brought against them, were compelled to combine and put down the democracy. The democracy at Heraclea was overthrown shortly after the foundation of the colony by the injustice of the demagogues, which drove out the notables, who came back in a body and put an end to the democracy. Much in the same manner the democracy at Megara was overturned; there the demagogues drove out many of the notables in order that they might be able to confiscate their property. At length the exiles, becoming numerous, returned, and, engaging and defeating the people, established the oligarchy. The same thing happened with the democracy of Cyme, which was overthrown by Thrasymachus. And we may observe that in most states the changes have been of this character. For sometimes the demagogues, in order to curry favour with the people, wrong the notables and so force them to combine;—either they make a division of their property, or diminish their incomes by the imposition of public services, and sometimes they bring accusations against the rich that they may have their wealth to confiscate. . . .

Chapter 6

There are two patent causes of revolutions in oligarchies: (1) First, when the oligarchs oppress the people, for then anybody is good enough to be their champion, especially if he be himself a member of the oligarchy, as Lygdamis at Naxos, who afterwards came to be tyrant. But revolutions which commence outside the governing class may be further subdivided. Sometimes, when the government is very exclusive, the revolution is brought about by persons of the wealthy class who are excluded, as happened at Massalia and Istros and Heraclea, and other cities. Those who had no share in the government created a disturbance, until first the elder brothers, and then the younger, were admitted; for in some places father and son, in others elder and younger brothers, do not hold office together. At Massalia the oligarchy became more like a constitutional government, but at Istros ended in a democracy, and at Heraclea was enlarged to 600. At Cnidos, again, the oligarchy underwent a considerable change. For the notables fell out among themselves, because only a few shared in the government; there existed among them the rule already mentioned, that father and son not hold office together, and, if there were several brothers, only the eldest was admitted. The people took advantage of the quarrel, and choosing one of the notables to be their leader, attacked and conquered the oligarchs, who were divided, and division is always a source of weakness. The city of Erythrae, too, in old times was ruled, and ruled well, by the Basilidae, but the people took offence at the narrowness of the oligarchy and changed the constitution. (2)

Of internal causes of revolutions in oligarchies another is the personal rivalry of the oligarchs, which leads them to play the demagogue.

Chapter II

And they are preserved, to speak generally, by the opposite causes; or, if we consider them separately, (1) royalty is preserved by the limitation of its powers. The more restricted the functions of kings, the longer their power will last unimpaired; for then they are more moderate and not so despotic in their ways; and they are less envied by their subjects. This is the reason why the kingly office has lasted so long among the Molossians. And for a similar reason it has continued among the Lacedaemonians, because there it was always divided between two, and afterwards further limited by Theopompus in various respects, more particularly by the establishment of the Ephoralty. He diminished the power of the kings, but established on a more lasting basis the kingly office, which was thus made in a certain sense not less, but greater. There is a story that when his wife once asked him whether he was not ashamed to leave to his sons a royal power which was less than he had inherited from his father, "No indeed," he replied, "for the power which I leave to them will be more lasting."

As to (2) tyrannies, they are preserved in two most opposite ways. One of them is the old traditional method in which most tyrants administer their government. Of such arts Periander of Corinth is said to have been the great master, and many similar devices may be gathered from the Persians in the administration of their government. There are firstly the prescriptions mentioned some distance back, for the preservation of a tyranny, in so far as this is possible; viz. that the tyrant should lop off those who are too high; he must put to death men of spirit; he must not allow common meals, clubs, education, and the like; he must be upon his guard against anything which is likely to inspire either courage or confidence among his subjects; he must prohibit literary assemblies or other meetings for discussion, and he must take every means to prevent people from knowing one another (for acquaintance begets mutual confidence). Further, he must compel all persons staying in the city to appear in public and live at his gates; then he will know what they are doing: if they are always kept under, they will learn to be humble. In short, he should practise these and the like Persian and barbaric arts, which all have the same object. A tyrant should also endeavour to know what each of his subjects says or does, and should employ spies, like the "female detectives" at Syracuse, and the eavesdroppers whom Hiero was in the habit of sending to any place of resort or meeting; for the fear of informers prevents people from speaking their minds, and if they do, they are more easily found out. Another art of the tyrant is to sow quarrels among the citizens; friends should be embroiled with friends, the people with the notables, and the rich with one another. Also he should impoverish his subjects; he thus provides against the maintenance of a guard by the citizens and the people, having to keep hard at work, are prevented from conspiring. . . .

Chapter 12

. . . In the *Republic* of Plato, Socrates treats of revolutions, but not well, for he mentions no cause of change which peculiarly affects the first, or perfect state. He only says that the cause is that nothing is abiding, but all things change in a certain cycle; and that the origin of the change consists in those numbers "of which 4 and 3, married with 5, furnish two harmonies"—(he means when the number of this figure becomes solid); he conceives that nature at certain times produces bad men who will not submit to education; in which latter particular he may very likely be not far wrong, for there may well be some men who cannot be educated and made virtuous. But why is such a cause of change peculiar to his ideal state, and not rather common to all states, nay, to everything which comes into being at all? And is it by the agency of time, which, as he declares, makes all things change, that things which did not begin together, change together? For example, if something has come into being the day before the completion of the cycle, will it change with things that came into being before? Further, why should the perfect state change into the Spartan? For governments more often take an opposite form than one akin to them. The same remark is applicable to the other changes; he says that the Spartan constitution changes into an oligarchy, and this into a democracy, and this again into a tyranny. And yet the contrary happens quite as often; for a democracy is even more likely to change into an oligarchy than into a monarchy. Further, he never says whether tyranny is, or is not, liable to revolutions, and if it is, what is the cause of them, or into what form it changes. And the reason is, that he could not very well have told: for there is no rule; according to him it should revert to the first and best, and then there would be a complete cycle. . . .

BOOK VI

Chapter 2

The basis of a democratic state is liberty; which, according to the common opinion of men, can only be enjoyed in such a state;—this they affirm to be the great end of every democracy. One principle of liberty is for all to rule and be ruled in turn, and indeed democratic justice is the application of numerical not proportionate equality; whence it follows that the majority must be supreme, and that whatever the majority approve must be the end and the just. Every citizen, it is said, must have equality, and therefore in a democracy the poor have more power than the rich, because there are more of them, and the will of the majority is supreme. This, then, is one note of liberty which all democrats affirm to be the principle of their state. Another is that a man should live as he likes. This, they say, is the privilege of a free-man, since, on the other hand, not to live as a man likes is the mark of a slave. This is the second characteristic of democracy, whence has arisen the claim of men to be ruled by none, if possible, or, if this is impossible, to rule and be ruled in turns; and so it contributes to the freedom based upon equality. . . .

Chapter 6

. . . The first and best attempered of oligarchies is akin to a constitutional government. In this there ought to be two standards of qualification; the one high, the other low—the lower qualifying for the humbler yet indispensable offices and the higher for the superior ones. He who acquires the prescribed qualification should have the rights of citizenship. The number of those admitted should be such as will make the entire governing body stronger than those who are excluded, and the new citizen should be always taken out of the better class of the people. The principle, narrowed a little, gives another form of oligarchy; until at length we reach the most cliquish and tyrannical of them all, answering to the extreme democracy, which, being the worst, requires vigilance in proportion to its badness. For as healthy bodies and ships well provided with sailors may undergo many mishaps and survive them, whereas sickly constitutions and rotten ill-manned ships are ruined by the very least mistake, so do the worst forms of government require the greatest care. The populousness of democracies generally preserves them (for number is to democracy in the place of justice based on proportion); whereas the preservation of an oligarchy clearly depends on an opposite principle, viz. good order.

BOOK VII

Chapter I

He who would duly inquire about the best form of a state ought first to determine which is the most eligible life; while this remains uncertain the best form of the state must also be uncertain; for, in the natural order of things, those may be expected to lead the best life who are governed in the best manner of which their circumstances admit. We ought therefore to ascertain, first of all, which is the most generally eligible life, and then whether the same life is or is not best for the state and for individuals.

Assuming that enough has been already said in discussions outside the school concerning the best life, we will now only repeat what is contained in them. Certainly no one will dispute the propriety of that partition of goods which separates them into three classes, viz. external goods, goods of the body, and goods of the soul, or deny that the happy man must have all three. For no one would maintain that he is happy who has not in him a particle of courage or temperance or justice or prudence, who is afraid of every insect which flutters past him, and will commit any crime, however great, in order to gratify his lust of meat or drink, who will sacrifice his dearest friend for the sake of half-a-farthing, and is as feeble and false in mind as a child or a madman. These propositions are almost universally acknowledged as soon as they are uttered, but men differ about the degree or relative superiority of this or that good. Some think that a very moderate amount of virtue is enough, but set no limit to their desires of wealth, property, power, reputation, and the like. To whom we reply by an appeal to facts, which easily prove that mankind do not acquire or preserve virtue by the help of external goods, but external goods by the help of virtue, and that happiness, whether consisting in pleasure or virtue, or both, is more often found with those who are most highly cultivated in their mind and in their character, and have only a moderate share of external goods, than among those who possess external goods to a useless extent but are deficient in higher qualities; and this is not only matter of experience, but, if reflected upon, will easily appear to be in accordance with reason. For, whereas external goods have a limit, like any other instrument, and all things useful are of such a nature that where there is too much of them they must either do harm, or at any rate be of no use, to their possessors, every good of the soul, the greater it is, is also of greater use, if the epithet useful as well as noble is appropriate to such subjects. No proof is required to show that the best state of one thing in relation to another corresponds in degree of excellence to the interval between the natures of which we say that these very states are states: so that, if the soul is more noble than our possessions or our bodies, both absolutely and in relation to us, it must be admitted that the best state of either has a similar ratio to the other. Again, it is for the sake of the soul that goods external and goods of the body are eligible at all, and all wise men ought to choose them for the sake of the soul, and not the soul for the sake of them.

Let us acknowledge then that each one has just so much of happiness as he has of virtue and wisdom, and of virtuous and wise action. God is a witness to us of this truth, for he is happy and blessed, not by reason of any external good, but in himself and by reason of his own nature. And herein of necessity lies the difference between good fortune and happiness; for external goods come of themselves, and chance is the author of them, but no one is just or temperate by or through chance. In like manner, and by a similar train of argument, the happy state may be shown to be that which is best and which acts rightly; and rightly it cannot act without doing right actions, and neither individual nor state can do right actions without virtue and wisdom. Thus the courage, justice, and wisdom of a state have the same form and nature as the qualities which give the individual who possesses them the name of just, wise, or temperate.

Thus much may suffice by way of preface: for I could not avoid touching upon these questions, neither could I go through all the arguments affecting them; these are the business of another science.

Let us assume then that the best life, both for individuals and states, is the life of virtue, when virtue has external goods enough for the performance of good actions. If there are any who controvert our assertion, we will in this treatise pass them over, and consider their objections hereafter.

Chapter 2

There remains to be discussed the question, Whether the happiness of the individual is the same as that of the state, or different? Here again there can be no doubt—

no one denies that they are the same. For those who hold that the well-being of the individual consists in his wealth, also think that riches make the happiness of the whole state, and those who value most highly the life of a tyrant deem that city the happiest which rules over the greatest number; while they who approve an individual for his virtue say that the more virtuous a city is, the happier it is. Two points here present themselves for consideration: first (I), which is the more eligible life, that of a citizen who is a member of a state, or that of an alien who has no political ties; and again (2), which is the best form of constitution or the best condition of a state, either on the supposition that political privileges are desirable for all, or for a majority only? Since the good of the state and not of the individual is the proper subject of political thought and speculation, and we are engaged in a political discussion, while the first of these two points has a secondary interest for us, the latter will be the main subject of our inquiry.

Now it is evident that the form of government is best in which every man, whoever he is, can act best and live happily. But even those who agree in thinking that the life of virtue is the most eligible raise a question, whether the life of business and politics is or is not more eligible than one which is wholly independent of external goods, I mean than a contemplative life, which by some is maintained to be the only one worthy of a

philosopher. For these two lives—the life of the philosopher and the life of the statesman—appear to have
been preferred by those who have been most keen in the
pursuit of virtue, both in our own and in other ages.
Which is the better is a question of no small moment;
for the wise man, like the wise state, will necessarily
regulate his life according to the best end. There are
some who think that while a despotic rule over others is
the greatest injustice, to exercise a constitutional rule
over them, even though not unjust, is a great impediment to a man's individual well-being. Others take an
opposite view; they maintain that the true life of man is
the practical and political, and that every virtue admits
of being practised, quite as much by statesmen and rulers as by private individuals. . . .

Chapter 4

. . . In what has preceded I have discussed other forms
of government; in what remains the first point to be
considered is what should be the conditions of the ideal
or perfect state; for the perfect state cannot exist without a due supply of the means of life. And therefore we
must pre-suppose many purely imaginary conditions,
but nothing impossible. There will be a certain number
of citizens, a country in which to place them, and the
like. As the weaver or shipbuilder or any other artisan
must have the material proper for his work (and in pro-

portion as this is better prepared, so will the result of his art be nobler), so the statesman or legislator must also have the materials suited to him.

First among the materials required by the statesman is population: he will consider what should be the number and character of the citizens, and then what should be the size and character of the country. Most persons think that a state in order to be happy ought to be large; but even if they are right, they have no idea what is a large and what a small state. For they judge of the size of the city by the number of the inhabitants; whereas they ought to regard, not their number, but their power. A city too, like an individual, has a work to do; and that city which is best adapted to the fulfilment of its work is to be deemed greatest, in the same sense of the word great in which Hippocrates might be called greater, not as a man, but as a physician, than some one else who was taller. And even if we reckon greatness by numbers, we ought not to include everybody, for there must always be in cities a multitude of slaves and sojourners and foreigners; but we should include those only who are members of the state, and who form an essential part of it. The number of the latter is a proof of the greatness of a city; but a city which produces numerous artisans and comparatively few soldiers cannot be great, for a great city is not to be confounded with a populous one. Moreover, experience shows that a very populous city can rarely, if ever, be well governed; since all cities which have a reputation for good government have a limit of population. We may argue on grounds of reason, and the same result will follow. For law is order, and good law is good order; but a very great multitude cannot be orderly: to introduce order into the unlimited is the work of a divine power—of such a power as holds together the universe. Beauty is realized in number and magnitude, and the state which combines magnitude with good order must necessarily be the most beautiful. To the size of states there is a limit, as there is to other things, plants, animals, implements; for none of these retain their natural power when they are too large or too small, but they either wholly lose their nature, or are spoiled. For example, a ship which is only a span long will not be a ship at all, nor a ship a quarter of a mile long; yet there may be a ship of a certain size, either too large or too small, which will still be a ship, but bad for sailing. In like manner a state when composed of too few is not, as a state ought to be, self-sufficing; when of too many, though self-sufficing in all mere necessaries, as a nation may be, it is not a state, being almost incapable of constitutional government. For who can be the general of such a vast multitude, or who the herald, unless he have the voice of a Stentor? . . .

Chapter 7

Having spoken of the number of the citizens, we will proceed to speak of what should be their character. This is a subject which can be easily understood by any one who casts his eye on the more celebrated states of Hellas, and generally on the distribution of races in the habitable world. Those who live in a cold climate and in Europe are full of spirit, but wanting in intelligence and skill; and therefore they retain comparative freedom, but have no political organization, and are incapable of ruling over others. Whereas the natives of Asia are intelligent and inventive, but they are wanting in spirit, and therefore they are always in a state of subjection and slavery. But the Hellenic race, which is situated between them, is likewise intermediate in character, being high-spirited and also intelligent. Hence it continues free, and is the best-governed of any nation, and, if it could be formed into one state, would be able to rule the world. There are also similar differences in the different tribes of Hellas; for some of them are of a one-sided nature, and are intelligent or courageous only, while in others there is a happy combination of both qualities. And clearly those whom the legislator will most easily lead to virtue may be expected to be both intelligent and courageous. Some say that the guardians should be friendly towards those whom they know, fierce towards those whom they do not know. . . .

Chapter 16

Since the legislator should begin by considering how the frames of the children whom he is rearing may be as good as possible, his first care will be about marriage—at what age should his citizens marry, and who are fit to marry? In legislating on this subject he ought to consider the persons and the length of their life, that their procreative life may terminate at the same period, and that they may not differ in their bodily powers, as will be the case if the man is still able to beget children while the woman is unable to bear them, or the woman able to bear while the man is unable to beget, for from these causes arise quarrels and differences between married persons. Secondly, he must consider the time at which the children will succeed to their parents; there ought not to be too great an interval of age, for then the parents will be too old to derive any pleasure from their affection, or to be of any use to them. Nor ought they to be too nearly of an age; to youthful marriages there are many objections—the children will be wanting in respect to the parents, who will seem to be their contemporaries, and disputes will arise in the management of the household. Thirdly, and this is the point from which we digressed, the legislator must mould to his will the frames of newly-born children. Almost all these objects may be secured by attention to one point. Since the time of generation is commonly limited within the age of seventy years in the case of a man, and of fifty in the case of a woman, the commencement of the union should conform to these periods. The union of male and female when too young is bad for the procreation of children; in all other animals the offspring of the young are small and ill-developed, and with a tendency to produce female children, and therefore also in man, as is proved by the fact that in those cities in which men and women are accustomed to marry young, the people are small and weak. . . .Women should marry when they are about eighteen years of age, and men at seven and thirty; then they are in the prime of life, and the decline in the powers of both will coincide. Further, the children, if their birth takes place soon, as may reasonably be expected, will succeed in the beginning of their prime, when the fathers are already in the decline of life, and have nearly reached their term of three-score years and ten. . . .

Chapter 17

After the children have been born, the manner of rearing them may be supposed to have a great effect on their bodily strength. It would appear from the example of animals, and of those nations who desire to create the military habit, that the food which has most milk in it is best suited to human beings; but the less wine the better, if they would escape diseases. Also all the motions to which children can be subjected at their early age are very useful. But in order to preserve their tender limbs from distortion, some nations have had recourse to mechanical appliances which straighten their bodies. To accustom children to the cold from their earliest years is also an excellent practice, which greatly conduces to health, and hardens them for military service. Hence many barbarians have a custom of plunging their children at birth into a cold stream; others, like the Celts, clothe them in a light wrapper only. For human nature should be early habituated to endure all which by habit it can be made to endure; but the process must be gradual. And children, from their natural warmth, may be easily trained to bear cold. Such care should attend them in the first stage of life.

The next period lasts to the age of five; during this no demand should be made upon the child for study or labour, lest its growth be impeded; and there should be sufficient motion to prevent the limbs from being inactive. This can be secured, among other ways, by amusement, but the amusement should not be vulgar or tiring or effeminate. The Directors of Education, as they are termed, should be careful what tales or stories the children hear, for all such things are designed to prepare the way for the business of later life, and should be for the most part imitations of the occupations which they will hereafter pursue in earnest. Those are wrong who in their laws attempt to check the loud crying and screaming of children, for these contribute towards their growth, and, in a manner, exercise their bodies. Straining the voice has a strengthening effect similar to that produced by the retention of the breath in violent exertions. The Directors of Education should have an eye to their bringing up, and in particular should take care that they are left as little as possible with slaves. For until they are seven years old they must live at home; and therefore, even at this early age, it is to be expected that they should acquire a taint of meanness from what they hear and see. Indeed, there is nothing which the legislator should be more careful to drive away than indecency of speech; for the light utterance of shameful words leads soon to shameful actions. The young especially should never be allowed to repeat or hear anything of the sort. A freeman who is found saying or doing what is forbidden, if he be too young as yet to have the privilege of reclining at the public tables, should be disgraced and beaten, and an elder person degraded as his slavish conduct deserves. And since we do not allow improper language, clearly we should also banish pictures or speeches from the stage which are indecent. Let the rulers take care that there be no image or picture representing unseemly actions, except in the temples of those Gods at whose festivals the law permits even ribaldry, and whom the law also permits to be worshipped by persons of mature age on behalf of themselves, their children, and their wives. But the legislator should not allow youth to be spectators of iambi or of comedy until they are of an age to sit at the public tables and to drink strong wine; by that time education will have armed them against the evil influences of such representations. . . .

BOOK VIII

Chapter I

No one will doubt that the legislator should direct his attention above all to the education of youth; for the neglect of education does harm to the constitution. The citizen should be moulded to suit the form of government under which he lives. For each government has a peculiar character which originally formed and which continues to preserve it. The character of democracy creates democracy, and the character of oligarchy creates oligarchy; and always the better the character, the better the government.

Again, for the exercise of any faculty or art a previous training and habituation are required; clearly therefore for the practice of virtue. And since the whole city has one end, it is manifest that education should be one and the same for all, and that it should be public, and not private—not as at present, when every one looks after his own children separately, and gives them separate instruction of the sort which he thinks best; the training in things which are of common interest should be the same for all. Neither must we suppose that any one of the citizens belongs to himself, for they all belong to the state, and are each of them a part of the state, and the care of each part is inseparable from the care of the whole. In this particular as in some others the Lacedaemonians are to be praised, for they take the greatest pains about their children, and make education the business of the state.

Chapter 2

That education should be regulated by law and should be an affair of state is not to be denied, but what should be the character of this public education, and how young persons should be educated, are questions which remain to be considered. As things are, there is disagreement about the subjects. For mankind are by no means agreed about the things to be taught, whether we look to virtue or the best life. Neither is it clear whether education is more concerned with intellectual or with moral virtue. The existing practice is perplexing; no one knows on what principle we should proceed—should the useful in life, or should virtue, or should the higher knowledge, be the aim of our training; all three opinions have been entertained. Again, about the means there is no agreement; for different persons, starting with different ideas about the nature of virtue, naturally disagree about the practice of it. There can be no doubt that children should be taught those useful things which are really necessary, but not all useful things; for occupations are divided into liberal and illiberal; and to young children should be imparted only such kinds of knowledge as will be useful to them without vulgarizing them. And any occupation, art, or science, which makes the body or soul or mind of the freeman less fit for the practice or exercise of virtue, is vulgar; wherefore we call those arts vulgar which tend to deform the body, and likewise all paid employments, for they absorb and degrade the mind. There are also some liberal arts quite proper for a freeman to acquire, but only in a certain degree, and if he attend to them too closely, in order to attain perfection in them, the same evil effects will follow. The object also which a man sets before him makes a great difference; if he does or learns anything for his own sake or for the sake of his friends, or with a view to excellence, the action will not appear illiberal; but if done for the sake of others, the very same action will be thought menial and servile. The received subjects of instruction, as I have already remarked, are partly of a liberal and partly of an illiberal character.

Chapter 3

The customary branches of education are in number four; they are—(I) reading and writing, (2) gymnastic exercises, (3) music, to which is sometimes added (4) drawing. Of these, reading and writing and drawing are regarded as useful for the purposes of life in a variety of ways, and gymnastic exercises are thought to infuse courage. Concerning music a doubt may be raised—in our own day most men cultivate it for the sake of pleasure, but originally it was included in education, because nature herself, as has been often said, requires that we should be able, not only to work well, but to use leisure well; for, as I must repeat once again, the first principle of all action is leisure. Both are required, but leisure is better than occupation and is its end; and therefore the question must be asked, what ought we to do when at leisure? Clearly we ought not to be amusing ourselves, for then amusement would be the end of life. But if this is inconceivable, and amusement is needed more amid serious occupations than at other times (for he who is hard at work has need of relaxation, and amusement gives relaxation, whereas occupation is always accompanied with exertion and effort), we should introduce amusements only at suitable times, and they should be our medicines, for the emotion which they create in the soul is a relaxation, and from the pleasure we obtain rest. But leisure of itself gives pleasure and happiness and enjoyment of life, which are experienced, not by the busy man, but by those who have leisure. For he who is occupied has in view some end which he has not attained; but happiness is an end, since all men deem it to be accompanied with pleasure and not with pain. This pleasure, however, is regarded differently by different persons, and varies according to the habit of individuals; the pleasure of the best man is the best, and springs from the noblest sources. It is clear then that there are branches of learning and education which we must study merely with a view to leisure spent in intellectual activity, and these are to be valued for their own sake; whereas those kinds of knowledge which are useful in business are to be deemed necessary, and exist for the sake of other things. And therefore our fathers admitted music into education, not on the ground either of its necessity or utility, for it is not necessary, nor indeed useful in the same manner as reading and writing, which are useful in money-making, in the management of a household, in the acquisition of knowledge and in political life, nor like drawing, useful for a more correct judgement of the works of artists, nor again like gymnastic, which gives health and strength; for neither of these is to be gained from music. There remains, then, the use of music for intellectual enjoyment in leisure; which is in fact evidently the reason of its introduction, this being one of the ways in which it is thought that a freeman should pass his leisure; as Homer says—

> "But he who alone should be called to the pleasant feast,"

and afterwards he speaks of others whom he describes as inviting

> "The bard who would delight them all."

And in another place Odysseus says there is no better way of passing life than when men's hearts are merry and

> "The banqueters in the hall, sitting in order, hear the voice of the minstrel."

It is evident, then, that there is a sort of education in which parents should train their sons, not as being useful or necessary, but because it is liberal or noble. Whether this is of one kind only, or of more than one, and if so, what they are, and how they are to be imparted, must hereafter be determined. Thus much we are now in a position to say, that the ancients witness to us; for their opinion may be gathered from the fact that music is one of the received and traditional branches of education. Further, it is clear that children should be instructed in some useful things—for example, in reading and writing—not only for their usefulness, but also because many other sorts of knowledge are acquired through them. With a like view they may be taught drawing, not to prevent their making mistakes in their own purchases, or in order that they may not be imposed upon in the buying or selling of articles, but perhaps rather because it makes them judges of the beauty of the human form. To be always seeking after the useful does not become free and exalted souls. Now it is clear that in education practice must be used before theory, and the body be trained before the mind; and therefore boys should be handed over to the trainer, who creates in them the proper habit of body, and to the wrestling-master, who teaches them their exercises.

Chapter 4

Of those states which in our own day seem to take the greatest care of children, some aim at producing in them an athletic habit, but they only injure their forms and stunt their growth. Although the Lacedaemonians have not fallen into this mistake, yet they brutalize their children by laborious exercises which they think will make them courageous. But in truth, as we have often repeated, education should not be exclusively, or principally, directed to this end. And even if we suppose the Lacedaemonians to be right in their end, they do not attain it. For among barbarians and among animals courage is found associated, not with the greatest ferocity, but with a gentle and lion-like temper. There are many races who are ready enough to kill and eat men, such as the Achaeans and Heniochi, who both live about the Black Sea; and there are other mainland tribes, as bad or worse, who all live by plunder, but have no courage. It is notorious that the Lacedaemonians themselves, while they alone were assiduous in their laborious drill, were superior to others, but now they are beaten both in war and gymnastic exercises. For their ancient superiority did not depend on their mode of training their youth, but only on the circumstance that they trained them when their only rivals did not. Hence we may infer that what is noble, not what is brutal, should have the first place; no wolf or other wild animal will face a really noble danger; such dangers are for the brave man. And parents who devote their children to gymnastics while they neglect their necessary education, in reality vulgarize them; for they make them useful to the art of statesmanship in one quality only, and even in this the argument proves them to be inferior to others. We should judge the Lacedaemonians not from what they have been, but from what they are; for now they have rivals who compete with their education; formerly they had none.

It is an admitted principle, that gymnastic exercises should be employed in education, and that for children they should be of a lighter kind, avoiding severe diet or painful toil, lest the growth of the body be impaired. The evil of excessive training in early years is strikingly proved by the example of the Olympic victors; for not more than two or three of them have gained a prize both as boys and as men; their early training and severe gymnastic exercises exhausted their constitutions. When boyhood is over, three years should be spent in other studies; the period of life which follows may then be devoted to hard exercise and strict diet. Men ought not to labour at the same time with their minds and with their bodies; for the two kinds of labour are opposed to one another; the labour of the body impedes the mind, and the labour of the mind the body.

About the Author

❧

ALAN RYAN was born in London in 1940 and educated at Oxford University, where he taught for many years. He was professor of politics at Princeton University from 1988 to 1996, and warden of New College, Oxford University, and professor of political theory from 1996 until 2009. He is the author of *The Philosophy of John Stuart Mill*, *The Philosophy of the Social Sciences*, *J. S. Mill*, *Property and Political Theory*, *Betrand Russell: A Political Life*, *John Dewey and the High Tide of American Liberalism*, *Liberal Anxieties and Liberal Education*, and *On Politics*. He is married to Kate Ryan and lives in Princeton, New Jersey.

DATE DUE

MAY - - 2014